Sean's Book

By the same author

Sean's Book

by Sean Hughes

There's more to life than books you know,
but not much more.

Morrissey

PAVILION

For
anybody I have encountered and could have been
kinder to, I dedicate these ramblings

First published in Great Britain in 1993 by
PAVILION BOOKS LIMITED
26 Upper Ground, London SE1 9PD

This edition published in 1994

Text copyright © Sean Hughes 1993

The moral right of the author has been asserted

A CIP catalogue record for this book
is available from the British Library

ISBN 1 85793 465 2

Filmset by Selwood Systems, Midsomer Norton
Printed and bound in Great Britain by
Butler & Tanner Ltd, Frome and London

2 4 6 8 10 9 7 5 3 1

Versions of these pieces have appeared in the
following publications:

'Winning Awards' in *Guardian*, 1 September 1990;
'Comedy is the New Rock and Roll?' in *Vox*, May 1993;
'Melbourne '91' in *Guardian*, 11 May 1991;
'Melbourne '93' in *Vox*, August 1993 and
'Being Irish in London' in *Irish Sunday Times*,
18 April 1993.

This book may be ordered by post
direct from the publisher. Please
contact the Marketing Department.
But try your bookshop first.

Contents

The characters portrayed in this book
are unfortunately just a bit too real
I only wish I could say differently

Introduction

Firstly I would like to thank you, the reader, for placing this book in your hands.

Secondly, I'd like to thank everybody responsible for enabling this to happen, from the trainee shop assistant who has put this in the wrong section making it nigh on impossible to find, to the old printer whose nasal hair has somehow managed to find its way on to one of the pages.

And fifthly, to the publishers for promising not to censor anything.

So why a book?

I have always had a love of books and when given the opportunity to put pen to paper, was determined not to bring out a coffee-table type book in the vain hope of cashing in on a saleable image. This is not a collection of wacky pictures of me sandwiched in between half-baked jokes soon forgotten about. This is something altogether different. Most will know me from television or as a stand-up comedian, well I can assure you that this is the same mind at work.

This book is where the stand-up sits down. It has been laid out in nine sections, under various themes, ones which I have dealt with in the past and no doubt will deal with again in the future. This time I wanted to create a more reflective mood, dig a little deeper, use a different medium. It is a mixture of poetry, prose, short stories and journalism. Essentially it is a book of moments, the tiny instances which make up our lives. I found, in my youth, I spent too much time looking for the big answers resulting in my missing out on many things, here I try to capture some of these points in time, to remember the past and as an aid to understanding the present. As a comedian you're always looking in, watching, observing, absorbing the culture around you, sometimes what you see makes you sick. We tend to use humour to pull us through these moments, we laugh out of despair, this seems to suit everyone fine, but when you see the same tragedies continually happening all of a sudden humour seems to belittle the situation. I do hope this book makes you laugh but even more so, that it brings out other emotions in you. I have always had a love of writing, I often find myself at home with pen in hand without realizing, much like painters who doodle. This is a collection of my doodlings. Please take what you can from this little venture of mine, but whatever you do, please don't let me end up being displayed in an Oxfam shop front with the history of the Swansea fire brigade and a Take That annual for company. That's all I ask and remember the joy of finishing one book is the excitement of starting another.

How to steal this book

To me theft has always been an under-rated art form. If I had my way it would replace the opera section in the *Daily Telegraph*, featuring anything from live reviews to the latest fashion accessories. As a wimpy young teen, sport was not my bag so I turned to crime. The very opposite to what most inner-city kids seem to do today. I started out small, the odd fifty pence from my mother's purse, for which I'm still visited by pangs of guilt, up to the full Christmas shopping list.

There are a lot of misconceptions about criminals, people think they have no morals yet I find them to be the most moralistic bunch ever to have the privilege of being pick-pocketed by. There is a strict code of conduct, for a start you don't steal for fun, you only ever take what is needed. If you can afford this book, skip this section and just rush up and buy it; you might well find me sitting at a table signing copies with a fixed grin on my face. My theory is that you should only steal from the big chain stores, they can afford it and in most cases their accounts allow for a certain amount of pilfering, five per cent I believe. Now I personally don't like the book-under-the-jacket or down-the-trousers method. In fact I find it a bit vulgar. The foolproof system is to be brazen-faced about it, grab the book, place it under your arm, pick up something inexpensive, a biro perhaps then proceed to the cash till. Buy the biro, even ask for it to be wrapped and believe me they won't spot the book. The cheekier you are, the better chance you have.

If this book is one of the many items you want to steal go into a department store, buy a hold-all, tell them you don't want it wrapped, grab your receipt, remember to place hold-all on your shoulder within their view. Then give them an 'I'm going to have a browse around your fantastic shop' look. That's a finger pointed backwards, half-wink, turn of the head to the right, look. When they're not looking, and at your own convenience, fill it full of whatever your heart desires. <u>If you're caught, just point to this section and say you're very</u>

<u>dense and that you were only following instructions.</u> See I've even underlined it for you.

If it happens that you haven't the bottle or are a born again Christian, there are legal ways of not having to pay for this book.

1 Pester your local library to stock a copy and when you bring it back put it in the gardening section. Statistics prove gardeners don't like my style of writing. This way you can take it out again the next day without any problems.

2 Buy it as a present for a friend, giving yourself enough time to read it first. Please remember while reading to wear gloves and don't dog-tail any of the pages and if you happen to spill coffee on it, pass it off by saying 'That Sean, he's always playing around with formats, he's a card isn't he'. The most important thing to remember is when the recipient talks about the various contents, act surprised, as if hearing it for the first time. You can even go as far as to say 'sounds great I must get a copy.'

3 Browse through it in different shops, the busier ones are the best, they tend not to hassle you for long periods and once they do, move along to the next shop or simply walk outside, ruffle your hair or stick a cap on, and resume reading.

MY

COMEDY

WORLD

*THE VERY
SERIOUS
BUSINESS
OF MAKING
PEOPLE
LAUGH*

Funny

The stand-up sits down
and writes some words
he realizes quickly
they are not jokes, just sentences
he perseveres
in earnest
until there is some soft form

These words make him happy
his jokes make others happy
a conflict of interest
a selfish self-analysis
a little depth maybe

On stage laughter rings through
it can be touching
we enjoy each other's company
I want to give more
out pops my little book of words
'Hi these are not jokes, just sentences'
the crowd laughs
he perseveres
the crowd laughs
in earnest
not sure how to react
we all feel a little uncomfortable
and that's how it should be
there's no need to be afraid
these are just words.

Winning awards

I was flattered when asked to write 700 words for the *Guardian* as it gives me the opportunity to use my entire vocabulary, twice. So here I am in Edinburgh, desperately trying to keep body and soul apart. What is the Festival all about? For performers it offers them a chance to try out new work in front of new audiences. On a personal level, it frees me to become Charles Bukowski for three weeks without having to write the poetry.

This year to ensure everything ran smoothly, I decided to keep to a daily time-table. This system fell apart when I realized eating wasn't on my agenda. The audiences in Edinburgh are, as per usual, a mixed bunch. In one was a brash American lady who burst in mid-show demanding to know who robbed her purse. It wasn't me. Still it's nice to know I've a bit of a following with the criminal world.

'Fame, fame, fatal fame,' a young Morrissey mused, 'can play hideous tricks on the brain.' I was told that I had won the Perrier Award as I walked off stage after another sweaty performance of A One-Night Stand With Sean Hughes. The judging panel rushed on to the stage to congratulate me. 'Will it go to his head?' I doubt it: if the panel had made it ten minutes earlier they would have seen two people walking out of this award winning show.

In years past I looked to the Perrier Award as a glamorous accolade. But since I won it, I think it can't be that much of a big deal. It will probably all sink in when I have a moment to reflect, but for now my show is the main concern. It's a lot harder to perform now as it has gone from people 'discovering' the show to the 'I don't know what all the fuss is about' attitude. But it's the same show.

Having received the award, I was told my life would change overnight. I was told I'd be inundated with big money offers, and invites to dinner parties with such notables as Simon Bates. The only message left for me the next day was from my flatmate apologizing for eating my Twix. As for dinners, I've just finished off a bowl of Special K. I didn't use milk, I used Perrier and I was listening to Simon Bates on the radio. Only joking, I wasn't listening to Batesy.

It was hard to celebrate on the actual night because you want to do something special; well, I've been drinking myself into oblivion every night, so by way of celebration, I had an early night with a cup of cocoa.

Oh but how my life has changed. Now when a person approaches me my hand automatically reaches out for theirs and I thank them for their kind words and try to figure out do I know them or are they just being nice.

So will television eat me up? I appeared on Channel 4 last week in a sketch, in which the cameras come into the dressing room five minutes before the show. In this send-up I'm nervously boasting about how great it's all going. Watching the programme at home are my agent and his mother. He's telling her how successful the run of gigs is. Meanwhile, the sketch finishes with me inviting the cameras into the show where we see there are only two punters. Ha! Ha! With this, my agent's mother turns to him and says, 'He doesn't seem to be getting much of an audience in.' Mass appeal. I don't think so. Well, all's well that ends.

Rejected comedy script

Once upon a time in the land of naivety, I was offered a five minute stand-up slot on some programme for BBC Northern Ireland. The thrill and novelty of doing live TV made me accept. The problem is that TV producers in general, if I may generalize here, don't have the foggiest notion about comedy; they know it's popular and have this terrible habit of calling it alternative comedy. I get to the studio to be greeted by two middle-aged beards; they want to discuss what material I will be performing tonight. I had been doing comedy for about three years, so I knew from the clubs which jokes worked best; one of my better lines at the time was 'My mum rang me today, she said she found my bed ... apparently it was on top of my porno mags.' The two beards decided this wasn't funny. 'That's not funny, do you find that funny?' 'No I don't, do you?' They muttered as if I was invisible. Once they had decided what was best for the night, they asked if there were any other questions. 'Yes,' I said, 'Will it be okay if I say piss off.' They looked at each other and said, 'It shouldn't be a problem.' 'Piss off,' I said. Retelling this story to a producer with a bit more suss, he said I should write a sketch around the tale and so I was commissioned to write a script about me telling a producer to piss off out of sheer frustration. Here it is.

INTERIOR: Two ever-so-trendy TV producers, Julian and Tristan, sit in plush office, Julian is on the phone. They are watching a video of Sean; they are completely stone-faced, laughter comes from the screen, this puzzles them. There is a knock on the door, in walks Sean, Tristan turns video off.

Julian

Sean. Hello Sean. We were just watching the video, it's a scream.

Sean

Thank you.

Julian [*laughing*]

'Thank you,' do you hear him Tristan, 'Thank you,' this guy cracks me up. [*Tristan laughs as best he can*]

Tristan [*laughing*]

'Thank you.' You're a very funny man, Sean.

Julian [*still laughing*]

Enough of that, Sean, what have you in mind for tonight?

Sean

Whatever you want really.

Tristan [*laughing*]

'Whatever you want really' . . . that's funny. [*He looks at Julian, realizes his mistake and quickly becomes straight-faced*]

Julian

Well Sean, if you could do a bit for us now!

Sean

Is it okay if I stand up?

[*Tristan keeps looking to Julian to see if he is laughing*]

Julian

Yeah, sure, we'll be your typical cabaret audience.
[*As Sean starts, he goes to the phone*]

Sean

My parents got divorced recently, they did it for the sake of the kids . . . because we hated the gits.

[*There's a three-second pause where there is silence, then Julian starts laughing and Tristan follows suit until the two of them are hysterical*]

Julian

That's funny, very funny . . . where exactly is the joke?

Sean

The parents got divorced because the kids hated them.

Julian [*still doesn't understand*]

O I see, maybe if you say it differently, something like . . . I'm not saying I didn't like my parents, in fact we hated them so much that we made them get divorced [*ignoring Sean*]... that's funny, isn't it, Tris?

Tristan

Yes, yes it is, maybe we need some sort of a gimmick. Do you dance Sean?

Sean

Not really [*he makes an attempt to swing his arms*]... no, no I can't.

Julian

A gimmick would be good, do you ever use fire crackers, dress as a woman, mis handle Teddy Bears, something like that?

Sean

Is it okay if I just stick to the gags?

Julian

Of course, yes... this is just something to add to it.

Tristan

He could spin plates...

Julian

It's been done.

Tristan

Not while on a motorbike it hasn't.

Julian

That's it, get props on to it. Now Sean, after the divorce gag, do a wheelie, then do a saucy joke then something a bit racy.

Sean

It's not really my style. I could say... I was with a girl recently, very kinky, she had really long nails... and a hammer... really hurt my back...

Julian

... Yeah Sean before you do the punch line... if you said she had really long nails and a big, er... , you know...

bosoms... without actually saying bosoms, just imply it with your actions. I don't want to tell you your job, you know how to do it.

Tristan [*on phone*]

Props can only get us a pogo stick, but they do have a Robin Hood outfit.

Julian

That will do, you can keep bouncing up and down, it will be very visual [*turning to Tristan*]... because that's so important in comedy, isn't it, Tristan?

Tristan

O it is Julian, visual, it's good for television.

Julian

So that's about it really Sean, just put one more gag in, a standard one, with all the bouncing and the canned laughter... that will be five minutes.

Sean

Is there no audience?

Tristan

No... we put the laughter in later, it's TV.

Julian

... One other small point Sean, your accent, those lovely sweet Irish tones you have...

Sean

Thanks.

Julian

If you could lose that ... work on a Northern club kind of voice, okay... it's going to be brilliant, because you're a very funny man. So have you got any questions?

Sean

Yeah there's one thing, is it okay if I say piss off?

Julian

Sure that won't be a problem.

Sean

Well piss off then.

[*We pull out to reveal that there is a film crew filming this scene*]

Director

Cut... that was great lads, it was ever so slightly OTT, if we do it once more, this time a bit more sit-com, let the audience know where the laughs are. O and Sean this time when they make the suggestions if you could accept them, I think that would work better. So... ACTION.

THE END

After submitting this, I shouldn't mention which company it was, but it was Granada. They said they liked it a lot but could I drop the 'piss off' punchline. Life imitating art or art imitating life. That's showbiz.

The <u>Comedy</u> Store

you, sit down, relaxed, with friends
to laugh
I, stand up, anxious, alone
to applause
I speak, you laugh, that's the theory
I speak, you heckle, that's the practical
I feel a tremendous need to hide
under my bed
the microphone amplifies such feelings
and sometimes you have bad nights.

Sean's Shorts

An account of the BBC2 series

As we finished shooting the series, everywhere I looked Michael Palin peered out at me, telling every one about his trip around the world: the interesting people he met, the little stories from the various places. I got to go to Norwich, I got to meet Stan the sandwich board man and then I realized, these were my choices. The way we made the programmes was quite simple, we all sat down, I picked six locations, they went off and researched them, I then took hold of the information, plucked out the interesting facts and created a little story. We had various themes running though the series. 'The grass is greener' theory was much in evidence, as was the protected regionalism people have for their home towns. The thing to grasp is that each British town is a carbon copy of every other, it's the people who give the town its style. It was also about our need to look for new things. We look outwards when we should be searching within. Unfortunately, the viewing public tends to dip in and out of programmes, thus sometimes missing the whole point.

We started off in London but actually recorded there last. This programme was the hardest to write because we're always blind to the beauty around us. The story went, I'm ill and unhappy, I decide to do something about it, that is getting out of London, but not before I have a theme tune and a dream about becoming a football player. Of course this was just an excuse to meet the Crystal Palace team. Sadly I seemed to have given them the kiss of death. I'm probably the unhealthiest person you're ever likely to meet and it was terribly embarrassing because when I was having a kick around with the players, I took a free kick and fell over.

So, off I go to the Isle of Mull for peace and quiet and to practise not falling over. During the first day's filming, I managed to fall backwards into a hole and gash my knee, my footballing career over. My lasting memory of Mull is best forgotten about, but I will forever remember the beauty of the Highland cattle and the constant search for vegetarian food.

Mull being a little inactive, I decide to embrace the culture of Manchester, one of my favourite cities in the world. Here is the perfect example of the people trying to create a scene where one doesn't exist. It's like a Hollywood set, big exteriors, no interiors. So we came here looking for IT, and what ever IT entailed. Of course we don't find what doesn't exist. To me, Manchester has some lovely watering holes, which I fell out of this time, a couple of average football teams, great music and a very violent looking bloke who called me a twat outside the Hacienda.

We were lined up to talk with Morrissey's dad. I was supposed to bump into him at a park bench, he would tell me who he was, whereupon I would ask him loads of questions without ever mentioning his slightly balding genius of a son. I had approached Morrissey three months previous to clear this little innocent scene with him, because I certainly wouldn't allow my parents to be filmed but we were only given word on the day of shooting, that he had put a dampener on it. For someone who expresses a gentle nature, I found the lateness of it all a bit rude. It was a pity as his dad seemed like a nice fellow.

On to Oxford to write my novel, another beautiful city. Oxford has some lovely bicycles, a couple of average bicycles, great bicycles and a very violent-looking bloke on a bicycle. The town is known for its students, who tend to be the butt of every comic's joke. I personally think it's wonderful that people have a quest for more knowledge. But there is something about Oxford which turns nice human beings into monsters of Nietzschean proportions, a little literary reference which only students will understand, so they think. I don't want to generalize, my bones are to be picked with the ones who think the importance is playing the role of the Oxford undergraduate. I have to be careful here as the ones I insult could well be my bosses one day, so they think. Anyway, I played the Playhouse last time I was here; afterwards a female student asked me in all seriousness, 'Did I feel inferior because I never went to university'. I felt pity rather than hate. I just hope she is sheltered from the harsh realities ahead.

Onwards to Norwich, a very pleasant town. There to sell our wares as it has the biggest market in England. Norwich has a lovely Arts Centre, a lovely football ground, tons of lovely churches and a mustard factory. When Norwich springs to mind, I will always think of the disco which was trapped in some sort of 80s time warp, they seem to be stuck in some Babycham era.

Our camera crew have worked extensively with Anneka Rice and it was an odd situation when people walked by the cameras, didn't pay a blind bit of attention to me but got very excited when they saw our sound man. Finally as all else failed I went to the Isle of Man to relive a childhood holiday which I remember as being very exciting. I must say, this time I found the place painstakingly dull which I suppose served its purpose as we were looking at the innocence of childhood. What jogs to mind is the bitchiness toward Nigel Mansell, go-karting, a café in the old train station, their homophobic views (homosexuality was illegal up to 1992 whereupon they ignored *their problem*, now there is a lot of gay bashing since they've acknowledged their existence) and meeting my first millionaire who wears wellington boots.

In all a pleasurable experience but it's nice to be locked away in my flat again. The only disappointment was not meeting Alan Whicker on our travels.

Comedy is the new rock and roll?

The music business is dead? I don't agree, it's only resting. So what can the press do in this situation:

1 Over hype anything reasonable
2 Give a free gift with the magazine
3 Pretend they have a Morrissey exclusive
4 Juxtapose comedy and rock

How many times of late have we heard comedy is the new rock and roll. The only link I can see is, comedians are getting younger and pop stars older, and the kids want their heroes young, they want to know that the person they're paying to see isn't going to pop their clogs during the performance. Think of the gamble of paying £20.00 to see Bob Dylan these days. The Stones only do outdoor gigs, on doctor's orders, the boys need the fresh air.

The truth is comedy and rock have always been connected, but they've got it wrong, comedy isn't the new rock, rock is the new comedy. This dates back as far as Lenny Bruce making the jazz musos laugh; admittedly this wasn't very hard, you just had to end every joke with the word 'cat' and they were in stitches, look to the 60s again, Smokey Robinson sang 'People say I'm the life of the party cos I tell a joke or two.' I have it on good authority that the two jokes he told were fairly dismal, one resulting in the heckle 'Don't give up the night job', thus ending Smokey's comedy career. Heckling has always been part of the music business, 'Get your tits out' is another popular one, this is used by the record company when trying to oust the less talented members of the band.

The record companies have always been aware of the money to be made from comedy and it is rumoured that Julian Cope was dropped from Island because there weren't enough gags on the last album. Julian disagrees: 'There were plenty of gags, they just didn't get them.' When contacted, his manager, Seb Shelton, speaking from his North London hideout, well I'm not sure what he said, as there seemed to be two Dobermen barking a lot in the background. The gist of it was, 'Yes Julian's funny, down boy, he's only here to read the meter, the hardest thing in this business is trying to, hold on, no they're friendly, keep a straight face... oh shit I'll call you an ambulance.' The phone went dead.

So what do you need to be a good comic? Material first and foremost. Blues bands are hard to beat for content... 'I woke up this morning, the wife was dead.' They're very clever, the build up is always the same. 'I woke up this morning' and then they list their personal tragedies. Andy White, the Belfast crooner, has a nice line in gags, 'My car has seen better days, none of them with me.' That's a good joke, but you need the confidence to deliver it, Andy bottled and smothered it in music, so it barely raised a chuckle. He needs a few more years in the music biz before he becomes a stand-up comic.

The catchphrase is a good comedy device, The Ramones were the first to use this with their memorable '1234', in between each song; they were also very keen on the running gag, playing the same song 120 times a night.

Audience patter is important. The Wedding Present are known for their in between song patter, this ranges from 'All right' to 'We don't do encores'. How soon before this develops into a twenty-minute monologue. Face pulling is a comedy basic but still a crowd pleaser, Tim Booth (James) is one of the better exponents of this art form.

The visual gag is one of my personal favourites, and there are few better exponents of this than from the Fatima Mansions' Cathal Coughlan. I recently caught up with him while running after him (that's word play, see rap). I spoke to Cathal in his Newcastle hide-out, firstly he was a bit pissed off because he hasn't got any dogs. Cathal takes his visual jokes very seriously, and is very proud of the 'drawing blood by banging the microphone against his face' joke, but his *pièce de résistance*, so far only seen in Italy (another comedy ploy, trying the new stuff out of town first) was the 'sticking a Virgin Mary up his ass'.

Bad language is another comedy yes, yes. Carter are very fond of this. Jimbob speaking exclusively on the phone to me, unless there were other people in the room with him at the time, revealed how the Far East tour went. Their opening gambit in Australia was 'Hello Sydney, fuck off'. It was a triumph, the next night they went for the subtle approach 'Hello Melbourne, bollocks', it didn't work, for Japan they reverted back to the tested material. 'Hello Tokyo, fuck off...' at which point the crowd did, you live and learn. Incidentally Jimbob hasn't got a dog, having lost one before, if you see his dog apparently it looks like Robert Smith and answers to the name Robert Smith.

The first bands to fully admit to the comedy link were The Higsons, The Results and The Fabulous Poodles, all disbanded now over comical differences. I rang Charlie Higson at his East London hide-out, which he shares with a cat, but he wasn't in. Charlie is best known now for his writing collaborations with Harry Enfield. I met up with Arthur Smith (ex-Results) and Ronnie Golden (ex-Poodles) in a pub in west London called the Hide-out, incidentally they don't allow dogs in, except guide dogs. The point is they are now both comedy gods on the club circuit. I put it to them why they left the music behind. 'I enjoyed the lifestyle, the money, the drugs and the chicks but the music was taking over the comedy' one of them said, actually it could have been me, the night's a bit of a blur now. So guys why did you even bother with the pretence of the music? 'Rockers get better advances,' they said in unison, or was it a unicycle, I must start taping these interviews.

So as established comics go on to do adverts, rockers sneak on to the comedy circuit, unless you're Lemmy, then it's straight on to the ads. It was inevitable rock was going this way; as a child bullied at school, you try to humour them to avoid a beating, have you ever tried singing for a bully... my point exactly. My favourite type of joke is the subtle one, the Stone Roses had the best one, where they sign to Geffen for four million and haven't recorded anything for three years.

People who pay to see me

I trust you,
you as a crowd are an individual
a multi-emotioned monster.
You cheer me and applaud
and I thank you.
I want to make you feel good
I want to mind-fuck you
and cater for your different needs.
This is not Showbusiness
I know this is just a night out for you.
I need this more than you.
I am one person
a multi-emotioned monster.
I cheer you and applaud.
At this point the people on the guest list snigger

The making of Sean's Show

Tuesday 8th June

It's Seanie's show la la la la, we're back at rehearsals. It's been a year since the first series. I took six months plotting out the story lines before I put pen to paper, or should I say finger to lap-top. When it came to the actual writing it only took a week per show. So this is day one, starting at 10.00 am when we all sit around a table and have our first official reading of the script. It's a lovely feeling seeing actors bring my words to life this is countered quickly with the realization that some of the lines are complete crap. It's an odd one as nobody ever tells you this until you change it then you hear a chorus of 'I'm glad that one's gone.' The blistering heat, a slight hangover, the caffeine-addled brain and the fact that the opening isn't strong enough makes for a busy day. On this day we just block out the moves while I pop up with new ideas as they come. We finish around four but realistically my brain is on call twenty-four hours a day over the next seven weeks. I had arranged to go to the theatre tonight, a friend had already bought the tickets so there was no backing out now. It's strange feeling it's more a duty than an enjoyment to go to the theatre. The West End seem to have a policy to play it safe by re-running old favourites rather than gambling on an original work. They will daringly show an anti-establishment play from the sixties which has no meaning to us now, and all but ignore the thorny issues of today. The saddest indication is that some of the fringe venues are following suit. The economics of the situation demand this, shallow types will flock to a safe well-tested bit of escapism, as the youth will gather en masse at a Bjorn Again concert. They both result in a nice night out, no surprises, no shocks. Tonight I see *Juno and the Paycock*, on the way I'm still re-writing scenes. Juno has aged well, the only off-putting thing is the way the audience feels a need to guffaw at the slightest hint of a joke. Later I go to see Carter The Unstoppable Sex Machine at the Camden Palace, the bouncers are kept busy all night with stage divers, what is wrong with these people do they not realize that swimming pools supply boards and everything? Anyway I have a sneaky suspicion it was the same four people all night.

Wednesday 9th June

Whenever I read a book I find myself relating to one of the characters. After reading Brian Keenan's account of the hostages I stayed in my room with the lights out for six months, so maybe I've picked the wrong time to read a biography of Montgomery Clift, the seminal New York actor. In it there are tales of his excessive lifestyle, the mood swings, the off-handedness and his difficulty to work with, I just pictured myself saying 'I said I wanted one-and-three-quarter spoons of sugar in my tea. Right that's it I'm quitting.' I come in fresh-faced with my re-writes, I notice a young woman sitting at the back of the hall, we are not introduced, at the end of the day curiosity gets the better of me and I ask who she is, apparently she is on work experience. I go over and wish her well in her career as someone with the ability to sit on a chair without moving for five hours. It's quite a talent.

Thursday 10th June

I'm awoken at 7.30 by the postman. The builder I had round recently thought it would be a good idea to take away the existing letterbox and replace it with one that won't take anything besides postcards. He is the inspiration behind one of our new characters, Bobby the Builder. Today besides rehearsals I have to trim a minute and a half off the script. My main ally is the director Sylvie Boden, she cares for the show as much as I do. This is a joyous rarity, everyone else works to the best of their ability, we all get on well, but the two of us labour as if our lives depend on it.

Friday 11th June

First thing we do today is run the whole show in front of the production team. At the same point workmen in the next building decide this is a good time to start drilling. We do a terrible run, I become worried and make severe cuts. In the afternoon the dancers come in, we watch what they have choreographed for my singing scene. For some reason I always get embarrassed watching people dance, over the two series I have never been able to look them straight in the face. When you're at home writing these scenes you tend to forget that eventually you have to film them.

Saturday 12th June

I had an extremely early night but this morning I feel absolutely knackered. We record today and we spend all day at the studio going over the show word for word for the camera crew. Their laughter is heartening. I try not to give the full performance until the night. Anyway it's hard to go the full wellie during the week in a room with a couple of chairs when you're sweating profusely from the heat. We do a dress rehearsal at 5.30, this goes well, then I go to get my picture taken with our special guest Bea Arthur, then Sylvie hands out notes, I eat a cheese sandwich and drink my 80th cup of tea for the day. I say hello to the audience and Mark Lamarr keeps them entertained between takes, our big task tonight is to divert them while we place Bea in position so the surprise isn't gone. Apparently when Bea first read the script she was baffled but after the recording she was full of praise. The show went well even though the audience were a bit slow on the uptake. Afterwards with the help of alcohol and the reliving of a year's work, I sink into oblivion.

Sunday 13th June

I get up do some shopping and seven days' worth of washing up.

LOOKING

FOR

LOVE

*THE CYNIC
KNOWS LOVE
IS A STATE
OF MIND
AND CAN
NEVER FULLY
EXIST, THE
CYNIC HOPES
TO BE PROVED
WRONG*

How I feel

You are more than a ray of sunshine.
I, a leafless tree, you an evergreen.
I tramp off the beaten path
in your forest.
You are the glimpse of the moon I seek
a shiny reflection on the water's skin,
you walk hand in hand with the stars.

I can pretend all I like.
The most romantic thing I can say to you is,
you're the one I want to have problems with.

A three hour wait at an airport

Susan, Emma, Jackie and Beth.
Where once there was a flame
now there is only a name
where once you were my very world
now a mere memory.

I look to the utter beauty of strangers
nameless people waiting to be tagged
dreaming of those times ahead
hoping you'll be the one who got away.

A what could have been, destroyed.
A has been seeming fresh.
Asking too much from too little.
Asking too little from too much.
At least I'm still asking.

For better or worse are the vows
what about indifference.

My pen pal

We caress with words
make love with sentences
fumble with question marks
hug with commas
say hello with capitals
lay together with punctuation marks
kiss with XXX's
say good night with full stops.
Add PS for some thing really special.

Shaking hands

After the cutting of the umbilical cord
you are never again as close to your mother.
Through your childhood your family are those blurred figures
you surround yourself with.
You crave love... silently and alone
you spend hours talking to mates
discussing how you can't communicate with anybody.
Somewhere, with someone, you connect,
there's a moment of togetherness,
enough to last a lifetime.
I have a friend.
That's all I need
just being there
not having to talk for the sake of it
you can get that at bus stops.
Just sharing those silences.

With time those silences have grown,
longer and quieter.
I can only hope you have a new friend
and not just a bunch of people you tolerate.

Loving the unlovable

The woman, out of sorts finds herself on day release, less frightened by the other inmates than of what others perceived as the real world. The bus journey there was helped by the glorious sun bouncing off the window, showing the grease marks from the sweaty palms of past travellers, crowded, she looked for the shade, she always looked for the shade. She didn't know why she was admitting herself, most came after a crisis, which symbolized drastic change. If anything she had the opposite problem. Her life had remained stagnant for longer than she could remember. Getting off the bus she cluttered up the place, apologies were mumbled, as usual she felt a nuisance to society. She felt a terrible guilt taking up the doctors' time. As the hospital came into view she started to practise what she would say. 'My problem is not having any problems.' She felt very middle class about everything, which was not the case at all, she came from a stable if not subdued background. Her present state was the result of a reliable, functional upbringing.

Walking along the smudgy white corridor, she recognized the smell without ever having experienced it before, with her forever now. Sitting down, stomach in knots, she picked up a magazine, the easiest within reach. It was a television trade manual. The ratings page showed that closedown regularly attracts an audience of over one million viewers; others would read this and laugh, she wanted to understand it better. Why did so many people watch it? Were they so bored with life they'd watch a still photo of a girl chalking a blackboard with an annoying buzz for company? Thinking it through she reckoned half probably fell asleep during an earlier programme, the others made love without bothering to switch the set off. It puzzled her.

Doctor Brown said it was natural to be curious, don't fight it, enjoy it. She thought that Doctor Brown was the first person to talk to her without a glint of future passion in his eye. He cared, that was the first thing he had said to her, 'I can't cure you, I can care for you.' He always spoke calmly, so calmly it often put her on edge. She listened to him, actually listened, not once did she find her thoughts smothering his. She was a child again, giving herself fully to him.

It saddened her later when she recollected that she had never felt like that as a child. Nearly always an old woman inside the child, mourning her lost youth, she had forever been suspicious of the intelligence of adults, of parents, teachers and policemen. She smiled a sad satisfaction that she'd been proved right. It wasn't so much that she looked up to Doctor Brown, she was just happy that there were people of his quality around. He'd set her little tasks in between sessions, to make her accept responsibilities. Although these seemed below her, she did them. 'Beginnings are important,' he had mused. 'I will put my trust in him,' she sleep talked that night.

He was aware that the woman's visits had doubled of late, he had stressed that she wasn't to become dependent on him, more frightening was the fact that she was falling for him. Flattering yet destructive. He wasn't one for steering away from problems, waiting for the inevitable, he was a confronter. She was in love with him, it was more a love people have for their pets. It was ironic that she wanted him to fall into her arms so she could protect him. Sex never entered her mind. She dressed smartly that day, perfumed herself, not for the Doctor, more for the novelty. She was relaxed and confident, new feelings for her, as she bounced down the corridor on a mission of happiness. She headed for the Doctor's office, more a poky corner which doubled as a cloakroom, she cursed the Government's handling of the NHS. That was another thing she loved about Doctor Brown, he had no airs or graces, no ego, if anything he played down his profession, even discarding the white coat, defiant of the old school, she judged. She knocked on the door, the Doctor was in place. They had their usual cup of tea, small-talked until it was cool enough to take in full gulps. She was overly keen to talk, it was strange, over the sessions, she had opened up to the extreme, but now she was chatting as if they were lifelong friends. He reminded her that she knew nothing of him. She started to probe, on seeing this he had to acknowledge that he could be of no further use to her. His job was done. She wanted to invent some new neurosis, but on remembering her state six months before was glad to concede that it was over. She was well, if that was the right word. Doctor Brown was fond of using the term eased, 'You have been eased, you have released yourself,' were the words they parted on.

This truly remarkable man, untainted by his education, had been her saviour. She waited at the bus stop, the wind affecting her ears and hands, the darkness toying with the grumpy commuters. The bus shoved itself into position, all swarmed around it, she managed to secure her favourite seat, downstairs, snugly in the back left-hand corner. The bus pulled away, the blue neon light throwing shadows at the tired dejected faces. A few hours rest before the next day's onslaught. These faces always depressed her, she could sense a pettiness surrounding their lives. But tonight she didn't seem to mind. She reckoned one of them could be a Doctor Brown, she would look more carefully in future.

Doctor Brown sat in his room staring into the middle distance, then one of the nurses came in to give him his medication. She told him it was time for bed, he wondered what he would do tomorrow. He had been sectioned three years ago.

Marriage

You give me this ring
a token of love
it shrinks with age
until it can't come off

I take this ring
a token of love
it fits perfectly on my engagement finger
maybe we're being a bit hasty

I give you this ring
a token of love
I see it by the sink every morning
at least your hands are clean

You take this ring
a token of love
handed down from my grandmother
you didn't like her much either, did you.

Poem 27, a recurring theme

A beautiful painting jumps off the canvas and comes to life.
It follows me down the street, it chatters at me.
I want to lie down
It lies with me
And starts to hug me
We are soon involved
sleeping together
I get used to the situation
They call it love... but
I find myself looking at other paintings
making excuses so I can go to more and more galleries.
I am a man possessed.
One night I get home very late
from a private viewing.
My boring painting is back on the canvas.
I notice things about it, I never noticed before
confused, I hang it in the bedroom
always avoiding its gaze.

A person on the street

Somebody is out there now,
looking photogenic
painting a beautiful picture with words
mirroring your good points
giving you a will to live
making it worthwhile
the story goes, we should meet up
fall in love, fall out of love,
depart, start. Again.

An emptier bed, the better the dream.
Stay away.
Please.
My love.

DEATH

OF

EVERYTHING

*LIFE IS
A SERIES
OF LITTLE
DEATHS*

Death

I want to be cremated
I know how boring funerals can be
I want people to gather
meet new people
have a laugh, a dance, meet a loved one.
I want people to have free drink all night.
I want people to patch together, half truths.
I want people to contradict each other
I want them to say 'I didn't know him but cheers'
I want my parents there,
adding more pain to their life.
I want the *Guardian* to mis-sprint three lines about me
or to be mentioned on the news
just before the 'parrot who loves Brookside' story.
I want to have my ashes scattered in a bar,
on the floor, mingle with sawdust,
a bar where beautiful trendy people
will trample over me . . . again.

Tribute to John Lennon

I want peace
You want peace
We all want peace
A piece of what?

We busy ourselves with rituals
until we forget what's important
It suddenly dawns on you
What am I doing about IT?
This thought is usually sandwiched between
'Did I put the bins out' and
'Is there anything good on the telly'.
Every little bit helps
even if it's only writing down a few choice words
to ease one's own conscience

Notes on dropping out of society

Dropping out of society has to be done during your late teens or early twenties, the ideal location is London. You have to remember you don't ever plan to drop out, it just sort of happens, you fall in with the wrong crowd, have financial worries or just happen to be wearing the right clothes at the wrong time. Clothing is very important, you don't ever want to be mistaken for a labourer, avoid woolly hats. I'd recommend cheap jeans, a very basic jumper, shoes on their last legs and an 'I've been to Florida' T-shirt. Dropping out of society usually happens overnight, you spend the whole night spending all your money on booze until you realize you can't pay your rent. When you've been thrown out of your digs you have now officially dropped out. You then have to find a squat. When you've done this, you can furnish it from Skip-U-Like. Once you're settled in, remember to drop back in once a fortnight to collect your dole.

The daily timetable on the other thirteen days is, simply get up around eleven, look for butts in ashtrays, have breakfast which is toast, then sit by the window and watch society. After a while you start to argue as to who is allowed to do the *Evening Standard* crossword, first editions come out about twelve. At 12.10 you have lunch, toast. Then you look out the window a bit more, watch daytime TV on your rented portable, which you've listed as stolen from your last address. Evening officially starts around three. You have dinner at seven, beans on toast. As you will have gathered, dropping out is very much like being a student, only the conversation is more stimulating and you read more.

So you're thinking to yourself this sounds like a good life, how do I go about it. To start with, stop doing whatever it is that takes up your day, move to a new town and when you've met a nice bunch of dropper-outers, hang out with them. Bonding occurs when you realize that you all know the lyrics to every pre-beard Elvis Costello song. It is also compulsory to use hippie-speak and you have to tell everyone that you love them on every possible occasion, such as sharing their last cigarette, doing the washing-up or if one of them decides to have a bath. It is vital to have at least ten funny stories from your past. These will range from your first joint, to losing your virginity to how you managed to get backstage at the last Clash gig. Don't worry about not telling the truth – you're not expected to. It is recommended that you repeat these anecdotes at every opportune moment, but it is considered rude to tell the others you've heard theirs before. You might think it's easy to drop out but to be let in, in the first place, you're expected to have absolutely no money. I find this a bit scary so it's advisable to have a secret bank account for those days when the others complain of pangs of hunger, you tell them you're going for a long walk to empty your head so it'll have something in common with your stomach (they love a little bit of poetry) when really what you're doing is taking money out and treating yourself to a slap-up meal at Burger King. Later, back at the commune you suddenly find sixty-three pence in your other trousers and you treat everyone to a pot noodle, that is unless, of course, you bumped into one of them at Burger King. Then you both suddenly find sixty-three pence and you share the expenses.

It is crucial that you build up some sort of tolerance towards cannabis. You'll find you have to smoke a lot of it while having those in-depth political discussions like 'Do you think that Kinnock dyes his hair?' It took us a month to come to the conclusion 'Who cares?' As you will have gathered, dope makes you apathetic. Don't smoke too much cannabis otherwise you'll never be able to remember this earthly experience or where your bank is for that matter. I personally consider three months is about the right length of time to drop out. Dropping back in involves telling some bare-faced lie making your excuses and returning home. This is not the end of it, you have to allow another four months to exaggerate your story to your friends and a further two months before you sort out the mess your life has become.

'Hell is other people'

'Another painless day of work over' he catch phrased to his chums as they stood in the crowded space of The George, a pub deemed okay for a quick one, before home offered a more comfortable seating arrangement. In fact, the pub had changed beyond reason over the last year, techno music blasted out, trendy haircuts scared away the tourists and the beer was warm. They talked about the day's events in their insular world. Kenton was always destined to work in television, the name was made to roll off the credits of every bland variety show ever made. To the outsider, working in TV must seem so exciting, little do they realize it's just an office job, a bunch of people gathered together to make a product. All pettiness no passion. Somewhat like politicians who enter their field for all the right reasons, only to be dragged down by the 'don't rock the boat' police. The lesson is never learnt – the trimmings are the trappings. Kenton was depressing himself, another drink was called for. On the surface he had all the attributes needed to be profiled in a fashion magazine: TV producer, a lovely wife Susan, huge house, expensive clothes, many trips abroad, member of several select clubs and a pretty good drug dealer.

And here he was with similar types deep in their shallow conversation, a group of men with a collective swagger to match. Drink was drunk. Four males plus alcohol results in the IQ being divided by at least twenty. They were at the patting each other's back stage, one more drink and they would hover above the ground, fancying themselves beyond reach. They deserved each other. Kenton caught the eye of a beautiful woman, well, more accurately, the lips. This woman had sensational lips, pouting, kissing her own dyed blond hair type lips. She was of the Wonderbra generation. She knew how to highlight her good points, Kenton was cynical of this yet couldn't help fancying her, he imagined mad fumbling sex with her. He saw her approach what he decided was her boyfriend. It annoyed him so to see a beautiful woman with guys he deemed below himself. Kenton had lost interest in whatever conversation he had been in, talking shop bored him, most things bored him. Kenton was now at a peepshow hunting out any number of feminine shapes, the open-cut dresses, the tight leather trousers, the fuck-me eyes, he thought he'd married too young, hadn't played the field enough but never had any intention of being unfaithful, Susan offered much more than sex but sometimes that was all he craved. He hadn't enjoyed sex with her for a long while. It was nearly dilemma time, she was having maternal instincts and they were both at the age where most of their friends were having abortions, and yet they never discussed any of this, such private important talks were kept for those beery evenings with the boys.

The bell called, goodbyes were slurred, the taxi journey a horny blur, Kenton got in the door, dropped the briefcase, huffed into the chair, flicked on the telly, realized quickly there was nothing on worth watching, missed the irony, washed his face, brushed his teeth, flossed his teeth, gargled between his teeth, admired his teeth, fell into bed, Susan was asleep, he was aroused. He hugged her, she didn't budge, he shifted around pretending to get comfortable, he kissed her back, felt her thigh, soon they were facing each other, both excited, Kenton kissed her lips pretending they were the ones from earlier on, he fondled her breasts, imagining he'd just taken off the Wonderbra, he closed his eyes and was now making love to the nameless person, it felt good, it got better as he took turns fucking the various shapes he had encountered earlier on. He still wasn't erect. His mind went into overdrive, in the middle of this mad frenzy Susan appeared, he was imagining having sex with the person he was actually sleeping with. This terrified him. He adored Susan and didn't want to drag her down with him. He tried to stop himself but his eyes refused to open and he was about to orgasm. It was torture as Susan, unaware of his hell, willed him on. Kenton came in his darkness. He died a little, a mandatory hug later he rolled over to his side and felt very alone, very troubled, very frustrated, very evil. What had he become, what had he let himself turn into, was he capable of love any more, had he ever been capable, had he just pretended that love was involved, something had to be done, drastic action was called for, sick of just letting things happen, it was time for change. 'I want a divorce,' Susan said,

The brothers

The five brothers standing in line
In their ill-fitting best suits
Guilty looks on their innocent faces
Dishevelled, yet shaved, yet unclean innocent faces.
These faces I've seen express many emotions
Here as a family for the last time
Standing in line, there to put their mother to rest.
All boys, I could picture them with youthful, hopeful faces
Being chastised for being boys
I wonder did they cry then
Different shapes, similar height, same shoulders
To think what was going through their minds.
My eyes flickered from them to her
If one cried, five lifetimes' worth would follow.
I cried first through the shock of seeing a dead body
Then I cried for my father.
There was no stopping me as I pictured myself
Looking down at my own mother.
I tried to meet my dad's eye
He was miles away, yet so close to home.
Later in the familiar setting of the bar
There was a respected hush
They were glass-eyed
Reliving the less painful of their memories.
I slept on my wet pillow that night
Wondering when they were going to give.

TRAVEL

*RUNNING
AWAY
FROM
YOUR
SOLUTIONS*

Plane crash

You're just about to die
And no one seems to notice
They eat their plastic meals
and sip their complimentary drink
While I contemplate my worth
I look at the air hostess
Her smile does not calm me
My leg starts shaking involuntarily
The person beside me starts to chat
I'm dying and he's telling me what he does for a living
At this stage I've smoked all of my duty free
It's funny how the smokers seem more concerned
about their plight.
I hear a strange engine noise,
The plane dips,
I smell fuel,
The plane shakes in unison with my leg,
Right that's it, it's over,
I look to my fellow victims,
They're on their pudding now
Surely they're just pretending nothing's wrong.
The captain comes on the intercom,
Telling us they recommend the Avis car hire firm
This must be code for the staff to prepare
for an emergency landing.
One of them stops me inflating my life jacket
and takes the whistle off me
The fracas stops my doomed thoughts for a moment.
I could've died of embarrassment.

A student abroad

Reflections of a Very Naïve 17 Year Old

The college term was up for the year and I had survived the party where everybody tells everybody else that they will be spending the summer in America and then stay in thinking of a valid reason on how you didn't manage to make it there after all. So after a night of beer, women and singing 'Let's go surfing' I still hadn't decided where my summer destination was going to be. That morning was my father's birthday and, being a student, I decided to use my initiative and knit him some shaving cream and matching deodorant. He said, 'That's all very well but when are you leaving home?' I arranged to meet what I laughingly refer to as my girlfriend. She turned up but her personality didn't. It was a typical summer's night, it was pissing rain. I was still weighing up the pros and cons of leaving when my parents told me they were redecorating. That was that, paint gives me a migraine. Dad dropped me off at the harbour, he'd done a fair bit of travelling himself and I'll never forget what he said to me on departure. He said, 'Goodbye.'

My plan was to be breast-fed by the British government. Plan A was to write in a bedsit and soak up British culture during the dark hours. So I left the dark ages and was shipped off to the twentieth century. On arrival, I sweet-talked some relations into putting me up. Once settled in, I visited a couple of hundred friends from Dublin, they all drank in the same bar. After the compulsory visits to the dole office and with the knowledge that you can't get a bedsit unless you're working, I decided I'd better get a job. I discovered quickly there were no vacancies in film direction and that Thatcher's job was very secure. (Phew, hindsight, eh!) I was willing to take anything. I was offered a job as a financial consultant for the Baker Street clientele. The only problem was I wasn't to get paid for six weeks. What does a boy with five pounds in his pockets do? He buys a tie, that's what. I really did think I'd be consulting businesses not a commission-only salesman. (Phew, hindsight, eh!)

I visited an old friend. He tells me I can start work in the morning for the Ministry of Defence. This boy goes to bed dreaming of the decisions he will have to make and of which country to blow up next. Getting off the tube that morning I had decided that we would reclaim the Isle of Man. But what's this, an apron? They want me to move cabinets within the building, while people with bowler hats make all the decisions. At least I've been given a false name by the removal firm, as it takes three months to security check people. Robert Fahy was my alias or, if we'd had a few drinks at lunch time, 'that little Irish cunt'. I worked with six others; one of them, Dave, was a heroin addict. I told him heroin was a life sentence, he said he knew that but was hoping to get out on parole in three years. He was Irish. Then there was Jimmy from Glasgow, he was moved after a couple of weeks, which was a pity as I was just about able to understand what he was spitting at me. He was Scottish. Another three were typical Tom, Dick and Harrys. Their names were Thomas, Richard and Harold. They were English. Then there was Said, he was a hard-working Indian. The others tended to give him a hard time. He kept himself to himself through choice. He was human. It was strange how, out of every possibility, I managed to meet every stereotype available.

After a non-eventful day at work my relations dropped the bombshell. They have decided to redecorate. Goodbye Auntie. Off to bedsit-land for me, that's just north of Kensington. Speaking of which, there is a very trendy market where all these very original people striving for individuality shop. So I thought to myself, that's the place for me. I dressed up in all my black clothes and strutted in. I looked around and my face went bright red, for there in front of me stood three hundred people with black clothes and red faces, trying to get out and be individuals elsewhere. On a day-to-day basis I'd get up early in the morning, doze through the day's work, chat about the football, then down to the pub and the last port of call was the kebab shop, for some food and a riot. I was just getting a feel for the place when the friends I was staying with told me they were redecorating. I booked my flight home. I said my goodbyes and everybody said they'd miss my cigarettes. On the plane home, after filling in my 'Am I a terrorist?' form, I was looking forward to the hospitality of the Irish people. The first happy face I saw on home turf was the Irish customs clerk and he strip-searched me. (It was probably Robert Fahy.) Mind you, that was the most meaningful relationship I'd had all year. Welcome back Sean.

My hometown

Many's the time, I would sit here
with my friends
and after a few pints
we would dream about our future
our hopes, what we would do
all our plans and ideas.
Some of us would act upon them
others, their hangovers would arise with the sun,
recovering enough to drown their dreams later on
pretending all the time that soon they too
would do as they had said.
a lifetime's drinking done in a lifetime
I go away and dream of our few pints.

I return, sober with success
to find my friends no longer my friends
just reminiscing machines
their stools now shaped to the curvature of their bodies
they know their place and I know mine
'If only' starts every conversation.
Unhappy with their lot
as am I.
I haven't the heart to tell them.
Through me their dreams are still intact
content with that knowledge
they don't need to know words like 'futility'.
We drown our sorrows
and I depart.
Again.

Melbourne '91

It's the Melbourne Comedy Festival and I am over here with my friend Matt, who needed a holiday as he is sure that he is about to develop a spot on his forehead.

The city is very laid back and has an air of wealth about it. So it was a shock to find they're in the grips of a terrible recession. You can tell a lot about the country by the recession jokes floating around. How do you get a small business? Buy a big business and move to Victoria. I'm sure the homeless in London can relate to that one.

The festival is five years old this year and getting bigger every year thanks to the hard-working and ubiquitous Tory McBride who basically runs the whole thing as well as getting as rotten as a chop with all the overseas acts. This was my first visit to Australia and I am already picking up the lingo. You hear about the beer-swilling yob who thinks Planet of the Apes is a realistic drama, but that is like saying all Englishmen are repressed about sex.

Monday
It took three days to get the show working. First major problem was finding out that my two-hour show was in an hour-and-a-half time-slot. Jetlag also took its toll. I timed the flight perfectly, managed to miss Easter weekend completely. Good Friday must be the dullest day of the year; there's never anything open. No wonder Jesus got up on the Cross – it was probably just for something to do.

Press night was a bit of a mess, it was like playing to 150

of those nodding dogs you find in the back of cars. They operate a 'tall poppy syndrome' here, which doesn't allow anyone to get too big for their boots. There only being a few international acts, they want you to know your place. It was all summed up for me at the opening press conference where I was virtually ignored by all bar one Smiths fan who wanted me to do his radio show.

Tuesday

Most days are spent doing radio interviews. Some of the disc jockeys are very stupid. Today I told one that I was very anti-drugs because I once OD'd on amphetamines, I was rushed to hospital and made to work the night-shift. Whereupon he said, 'Really, did you?' Australians have a habit of taking everything you say literally.

Wednesday

Tonight is the big charity gala for the Salvation Army. Here they do some good work with the homeless, unlike the ones in England who sing them a little song and say, 'Cheer up, will you?' I shared a dressing room with Terry Jones. As he changed into his black tuxedo, I was putting on my denim jacket. It was black, mind you. I took a strange and very tall American story-teller to lunch with Terry. We had a pleasant time. On leaving the American said, 'It's been an honour to meet you Mr Jones. And, oh, see ya Sean.' Certainly put me in my place.

There is a lot of good comedy coming out of Australia, none better than from Norman Gunston, famous for his in-depth interviews in the mid-Seventies. In one he asks Warren Beatty is it true that he has made fourteen films in the last fifteen years. When Beatty says yes, Norman asks him what he does for a living. One of the few things funnier is the price list in the hotel's mini-bar.

Thursday

Matt is in Sydney worrying about his spot. I am in the hotel watching in-house movies; caught the end of *Ghost* then went to the zoo. The only other zoo I've been to is in Dublin where they have a snake and a Jack Russell, but apparently they get on very well together.

The comedy festival clashes with senior citizens' week, so they've been putting on all sorts of special events for them like keeping the post offices open an extra hour. The city is very anti-smoking. I was having a cigarette in a public toilet and these two guys who were jacking up heroin said, 'Do you mind, put the cigarette out please. Think about your health, will you.'

The show is working a dream now. I've loosened it up and made it less intense. Got back to hotel and dozed off just as *Ghost* was starting.

Friday

The reviews have started to surface. They seem to like it but haven't quite figured it out yet, their comments range from 'slightly demented' to the 'new Tommy Cooper'. The best was after I did a bit on breakfast-time TV; the paper said I was 'as funny as a drain until I started doing my routine.' I did the *Steve Vizard Show*, a live chat show. Vizard wasn't there though; probably on holiday with Wogan. In this show they like their comics to do four minutes, not unlike the rest of the world. Doing four minutes on telly is like having sex when pissed – nobody quite remembers what happened, but you were certainly there and you think it was fun. I sometimes wish the mainstream would leave us alone rather than patronise us. Recently I was approached by the Wogan people who asked if I could be funny for five minutes without swearing. Notwithstanding many people told me I was brilliant on Wogan, I always say thanks very much, even though I've never been on it. Got back to the hotel and watched the middle of *Ghost*.

Saturday

The dreaded has happened – Rick Astley is in the charts and my friend Matt has developed a spot on his forehead. We were taken to see Aussie rules football – similar to soccer but with worse haircuts. The most interesting part of the game is when assistants of the coaches run on in luminous green trousers to give instructions to the players like 'hit them harder'. Only five more minutes of *Ghost* left to see.

Sunday

Matt's spot has become enormous; may need to be operated on. I have become obsessed with Rick Astley's latest ditty. We went in to the Megastore and asked them to put it on. They said they couldn't. So I told them Rick was actually outside and wouldn't come in unless they played it. Oddly enough they believed us and put it straight on.

We got to see some of the local sights. One guide proudly showed us his favourite tree. Pointing to the university he said with a straight face, 'I've never been to college but my parents have.' Got back to the hotel and saw the beginning of *Ghost*. Of course he gets killed; it all makes sense now.

Melbourne

'People like me need people like you'
Is what the young woman wrote to me.
I walk your sunny streets
Amazed by your fountains
Amazed that water is exciting me.
Melbourne
You embrace me
You ease my moods
You let me shoot my foul mouth off
You make me want to hand out gifts to passers-by

I kiss your city on the cheek
Your pores open up and let me in
Your love is sometimes overwhelming
Triggering off the odd moment of happiness
You hug me, make me feel wanted
You give me everything I could ever need
And yet it is only a fling.
Tomorrow I go back to what I know best
The cosy discomfort of London
Thanks for trying
Because people like me will
Always need people like you.

Melbourne '93

Monday (Some time in April)
Look up Comedy Festival in the dictionary, it should read: 'event held in beautiful city where like-minded souls gather, show off, get pissed, recover enough for their next performance; repeat until dead.'

Today is my day off, spend most of it waiting to be seated in a restaurant deemed cool by the beautiful people, eat, drink, fall over, play table football, fall over, tell people I love them, drink more, awake in bed, no recollection of journey home.

Tuesday
Steven Wright, the deadpan comic, is in town; his publicity states 'the Comics' Comic'. Tonight I have a rowing team in from Shrewsbury, my publicity now reads 'the Rowers' Comic'. I'm playing to an average of 250 people a night which gives me the opportunity to play with the audience and work out new material for the higher profile gigs back at home. I have to fly to Sydney at 7am to do a TV interview, fly back and then do my show so I promise myself an early night.

Wednesday
Get to bed at 4 o'clock. I'm scared shitless of flying, the way I feel this morning it would be a relief if the plane went down. Arrive safely, well that's obvious really otherwise the article

would have ended there and the mags would be running a 'Never reached his full potential' type feature and we'd probably sell a lot more videos. Every interview I do over here they want to talk about *The Commitments* – Was it fun to make? Well no actually, you end up sitting in a horrible port-a-cabin for eight hours, go out and say your lines and then back to the cabin, next question please. Today it's the Ray Martin show, the usual bland daytime stuff which I refuse to do in England, the studio audience is very diverse, they're all old ladies but the hair takes in all the colours of the rainbow, my kind of audience. I am very tired for my show, with my humour I don't like anyone to be the butt of the joke, at the start of the show you try to charm them, let them get used to your accent and then do your stuff. Tonight because of fatigue, my opening gambit is 'Anyone see me on the Ray Martin show?' 'Yes,' a pretty girl says. 'Get a fucking job,' I reply. It takes me about twenty minutes to win them back.

Thursday

All the reviews are very positive, sifting through the papers, terror of terror, out of the corner of my eye I see something that could probably affect the rest of my life Crystal Palace 0, Wimbledon 4 – relegation looms. I vent my frustration onstage by demanding the immediate assassination of Billy Ray Cyrus. This is one you can try at home: having a bad day? Write to your local politician, the 'Take Billy off the planet' campaign officially starts here.

Friday

Good Friday so obviously no Catholics in the audience, they're all at home kneeling in the dark, starving themselves to death in the name of guilt. I think my Keep Music Evil T-shirt and pale complexion frightened the front row tonight. I've always looked like a heroin addict without having to go through the hassle of taking it. And it happened again tonight, in a bar: guy wanders over, 'Excuse me, I'm waiting for the "great show" speech, have you got any drugs for sale?' is his sixty million dollar question.

Saturday

I go to a fun fair 'cos I'm a fun-fair kind of guy. Lost my hotel key on a contraption called the Zipper, it was hard explaining it to the receptionist. 'Can I have a new key? I lost mine while spinning upside down at sixty miles an hour.' If anyone is thinking of dieting, get on the Zipper as you can't eat for three days after.

Sunday

I've realized I'm one of those people who have a complete inability to shock. In my present set I talk about my hatred of organized religion, people trying to give their meaningless lives meaning by having babies and how relationships cannot work. There's me thinking, I'm rocking the very foundation of what makes these people's lives tick. Public Enemy Number One, that's me, and all the reviews say is 'What a nice guy, you can't help but liking him,' the most they could muster was 'He has a lovely warm cynicism'. So I don't think I'll be auditioning for Rage Against the Machine just yet.
See you back in Blighty.

Love

Sean the timid revolutionary

42 Wood Lawn Road

John looked at the floor of their sitting room; with the furniture gone it had no personality. The wine stain really stood out, he had completely forgotten about it but there it was larger than life, a constant reminder of their daughter's twenty-first. He remembered the spillage now, his wife Della poured white wine over it. She said that way it wouldn't show. She was wrong. This house contained a lifetime's memory. Della walked in. 'Do you think we've done the right thing?' she whispered. She always whispered when uttering matters of importance. 'It's only cement and wood,' John told her to keep her emotions steady. He laughed when he realized she was talking about the positioning of the settee over the years, not too loudly though, as he knew this was her way of dealing with the move. He had been treating her with kid gloves since the sale of the house had gone through. He was hurting inside as well but was expected to be strong, so strong he was. Their daughter had left the previous summer, the house seemed too big for them now. John had toyed with the idea of turning the second bedroom into a study, Della had argued that a retired plumber didn't really have any use for one, also times were tough, the recession had bitten, this was the first time government policies had hit them directly, and yet they would always be Tories. 'They got us into this mess, they can get us out of it' was something Della was fond of saying. A smaller house did seem like the right option. The extra money kept in a 'just in case' account. This was a new start for them. An opportunity to rid themselves of possessions they would have been too frightened to just throw out regardless. This process was helped when the removal man dropped the first load. After the initial anger there was a sense of relief. 'They're just things' it was delicately put by John.

It was a two-man job but they only sent one, Danny. On arriving Della gave him a cup of tea, which he dropped. 'One less thing to pack,' was his way of apology. He was one of those unintentionally funny people, 'Danny by name, Danny by nature' he would say as if it was the funniest thing ever. You couldn't help but join in with his playful laugh. He certainly made the move less painful. Mr Mirren popped in from next door, water was boiled, tea was drunk, cups were washed. Many a private moment was publicly eavesdropped over the years. They knew Mr Mirren would only leave after the kettle was packed. He would drink up to twenty cups a day but the caffeine didn't seem to affect him. He never had anything to say, that is until he was burgled, this was then his official story. If he could get it into a conversation, in it would go. 'I hope the new place is a bit more secure,' and away he went. John knew this story word for word, in fact, once at a party, stuck for something to say, he used it as his own.

Most of their worldly goods were in the van. The bigger items didn't cause any problems, it was the smaller ones that brought about difficulties. Della would pick them up, reminisce, cry, be comforted and eventually they would be packed away. Once everything was loaded, Della started to clean the house from top to bottom. John didn't understand the logic behind this but knew it kept her mind off other matters. She even had one more go at the stain, he drew the line when she started to shampoo the carpet though.

Moving house was the second most traumatic experience in life, John had read in a magazine. The article went on to point out the reasons for this. Things that wouldn't have worried him before now started to panic him. Making new friends, the slow process of getting to know the new neighbours, discovering the faults of the new house and the falseness of people who promise to keep in touch.

The last case was put into the van, inevitably this was full of cleaning products. The closing of the front door was their final task. Della held on to the knocker for longer than was needed. Now she was crying. Danny made a gesture to comfort her but decided to get in the driver's seat instead. John had a dry tear as Mr Mirren shuffled them toward the van. They silently agreed not to look back but Della caught a glimpse of the house through the wing-view mirror. It did look beautiful, she thought it could do with a new coat of paint though. Someone else would now live at 42 Wood Lawn Road, she hoped they wouldn't make too many changes. They set off on their journey, Mr Mirren waved them goodbye. 'What made you become a removal man?' John asked Danny, veering the conversation away from sentimentality. 'I always wanted to travel,' he said in all honesty. It wasn't long before they were at their new abode. They got out. Danny started off-loading quickly, hoping for a good tip. Mr Mirren was still waving at them. A new beginning for the middle aged couple, the new owners of 48 Wood Lawn Road.

The passenger

Being driven to distraction
Mouth open in splendid sleep
The motion of the womb.
The day-to-day sounds harmonious
Getting comfortable in cramped positions
the seatbelt keeping you in place.
I am light, a mother's heavy burden
A near accident sees her hand
thrust to the left
for reassuring safety
and then back on our journey
Letting the elements control us
and we're at the mercy of others.
Always.
What fun can the joy rider have
He will never know the heaven of
putting one's gloves in the glove compartment
or checking the wing mirror just for the hell of it
I'm pleased to say I don't drive.

A

LOVE

STORY

*THE HEART
BEATS ON
KNOWING AN
AFFAIR CAN
NEVER HAVE
AN ENDING*

Excited and frightened

Thoughts peter through of you in everything
Impossible to pinpoint with choice words
I will mis-spell words for you in haste.
It's funny, yesterday I was content
in bed alone, now
Telephone conversations are epic novels
Throw away lines, hidden mysteries
People get it wrong
They want to own others
I realize you don't even own myself
It's yours, in many ways.

You're not here, I carry on
A sad satisfaction hums above.
Keeping yourself in check,
'That's good' I say, noticing things
The trivia I so detest in others
is now a welcome distraction.
Wouldn't that be the way, without knowing,
this is the best part
Too busy rushing towards boredom
We forget this is as good as it gets.
maybe not.
I can't help but question even the questions.

Bliss in abyss

We met, liked each other
and arranged to meet the next day
I go to bed alone but happy
I awake in the morning with anticipation.
I think of the woman at regular intervals,
I find myself not looking at other women today

My mind races away with romance
happy thoughts flicker away,
I'm a nicer person.
I skip onto the future,
dreaming of a time when we know each other
a time when we lean on each other,
together for ever perhaps.
I arrive punctual, she doesn't turn up

If I see her again I will not bad mouth her,
instead I will thank her for
giving me several hours of bliss
in abyss

Late Night Telephone call

0   It's half past eleven, she's probably in bed

8   but I want to hear her voice

1   don't even think about it, just ring her

8   I'll have nothing to say to her

0   she never rings me

9   what if she has someone with her

3   I'll just sleep it off, no I have to ring her

1   shit, it's half past twelve now

8   it has to be done ... maybe tomorrow

Sleep

The sex god whom other men envied only slept
with women because he was frightened
of the dark.

Fooled again by her shapely ass,
curved breasts
and a dishevelled mind, yes mine.

I walked a thousand miles
and I'm still no nearer you.

Spending the Day With a New Girl

General looking forwardness
a tense moment of self-doubt in the bath.
'You're very quiet, Sean' she said quietly
there's no going back now.
Please don't hold my hand.
Struggle through until opening time.
Time please ladies and gents.
                    I love you, my little blurred beauty.

The rose

The ceaseless talk seemed seamless
Talking to the one you're with
while communicating with another
We both go home with the people
we love.
I feel bad as I make love while
thinking of this new person
She becomes an obsession
My loved one taken for granted.
To love two people fills you
with self-hate.
I rationalize, there are a lot of beautiful
women
None more so than my loved one
I don't want this to happen
it's funny how that line is
always followed by, it happened.
We talk, I find out things,
I thought she'd say
The predictability a fantastic insurance
Then she says it
I thought of you in bed last night
Aah there it is
we've already had an embrace.
Apart.
One too long.

Lover

She says 'It's over'
I put down the phone
It was the loudest click I've ever heard.
Boom and it was dead
then a deafening silence buzzed
around my ear
Finality can be so immediate.
I remember her trudging up the stairs
entering into the ozone
of my depressive atmosphere
The Cure tends to be the soundtrack
to my life.
I tried not hard enough
as did she
We could never play those faithful roles.

She appeared first as an angel
she left that way as well
I want to ring her now
tell her how I feel
and realize I already have.
And having gently shut the door
She wants to play in the garden
I don't want to play in the garden
to see her looking more beautiful
with another.
I sit here with memories for company
Knowing that if life were moments
                    we'd all have a good time.

Ex-

'Yes I think I'm in love', that's nice
You ask about me
this is the springboard to talk about him
Things you've done, that we didn't
I am happy for you, truly
We are still friends
but we reminisce less and less.
I forget we is now you and him
I want it to work out for you
by disappearing from view
vague non-details will suffice
no, no they won't
I want to know nothing.
You seem to be a different person with him
already these pointless thoughts
gently push through
Your closeness to him keeps me distant
Still near enough, squinting,
focusing, making sense of the blurred outline.
Then I realize that's how I felt
                    when I loved you.

Still

Struggling along with your shopping
the used carrier bag changing sides
as your feeble arms feel the pressure
Spotted in the distance, an ex-lover
Memories pound in
a thirty-second edited highlight
of what you now know was
the best time of your life
You remember the intensity of that love,
A love that saw you lose two stone
In weight
the shape of her hand is still indented
around your waist
your bindly legs curvatured still
to fit her princely thighs
The locket of hair you still keep
in a coloured box
which was also hers.
The hours spent looking at your watch
in anticipation of spilling out your
day's news
to your lover/friend/mother.
She meant everything to me
even more than life itself
see she even had the power
to push me towards cliché

We stop,
look at each other's noses
out of embarrassment
Notice little changes
Small talk
'I'd better be off' one of us says.
I get home
expecting to get depressed
from one of those
'What could have been'
self-pitying sessions
Instead I'm terrified
that four years is all it took
for this person to mean
absolutely nothing to me.

LIVING

ALONE

*MY HOUSEHOLD
APPLIANCES
ARE MY
FRIENDS*

Cooking for one

Meals For People Too Busy Being Miserable

BOILED EGG
This makes a delicious, light, refreshing breakfast. (Although an ideal breakfast, it can be made at any time of the day.)

SERVES ONE
Ingredients
1 free range egg
Salt

1 Turn on the cooker, by the time you've found the saucepan and filled it with water, the ring will be nicely heated.

2 Put egg in saucepan, it's likely to be in the fridge.

3 If you like, you can make tea or toast at this point, but it is optional.

4 Switch on telly, watch *This Morning* and by the time Richard and Judy have made you feel suicidal, the egg will be ready. If you like your egg runny, apply the recipe to Ann and Nick.

5 Eat.

You may laugh but I don't know how many times I've prepared a lavish meal only to forget to eat it. (Well about six times actually.)

Concern

Laying on the couch
doing the self-discovery bit
The phone rings
Alan's been talking out of turn
I go over to touch a crystal
The phone rings
Tina's getting a bit of a reputation
I thumb through my book on Buddhism
The doorbell goes
Martin's smoking again
It's time for bed
I read *Distant Voices* by John Pilger
Susie rings
She's concerned that I might be lonely.
'Yes I am,' I reply
and not a moment's peace
       to contemplate it either.

Too much caffeine

I sit down happy with my lot
Music fills in the background
Food heartily giving a sense
Wine oozes thoughts from my head
I have every reason to be.
For the moment I'm simply living.
I have a cup of coffee
I've got a good life... I think.
A thought makes me fidgety
I'm very alone
the music's too loud
the food's giving me indigestion
and the wine's gone to my head
now I'm trying to grab a thought,
hold it in its place, it goes,
another appears
things are getting out of control
SLOW DOWN PLEASE!
I want to be an old man
with many memories
Something inside me dies.
I have some cheese and go to bed.

Lunch

The quick lunch is essential for the fast nineties. Ideally you want a meal which you can make in the minute-and-a-half you have in between *Home and Away*'s ad-break and the beginning of *Neighbours*.

CORNFLAKES
This makes a delicious, light, refreshing lunch. (Although an ideal lunch, this can be served at any time of the day.)

SERVES ONE
Ingredients

Some cornflakes
350 grams of milk
teaspoon of sugar

1 Pour cornflakes into bowl, creating an even surface.
2 Pour milk over them in circular motion until milk starts to come into view.
3 Sprinkle sugar over flakes, using side of spoon, gently keep tapping while in motion. This will ensure that the sugar is evenly spread.
4 Eat, comment on how crap *Neighbours* has become, promise never to watch it again, then catch the second half of *Home and Away* at about 5.30 pm.

Home

Waking up in the morning
sleep deep and troublesome
hijacked by the reality of the alarm,
doorbell or phone.
The day consists of motivating oneself
talking, arguing, singing to oneself
the hand through habit, fingers the
remote control
after fifteen minutes you crave to hear
a human voice.
The slightly computerized telephone conversation
The feigned niceness of the shopkeepers' patter
The friendly nod to the recognized passer-by
Later the frank coldness of someone
you deem close.
I think of waking up with a loved one
making the effort to be human.

Chatting to faceless people about factness
results in falseness
you being an intellect know you are
the sum of the parts.
Home, double-locked into your castle
the sign reads
TRESPASSERS WILL BE TALKED TO
at length.
The moat's up
I pray for good swimmers.
You're alone, pathetic, weak.
A friend rings and I forget myself.

Being fortunate

Twenty-four hours can sometimes be just too much
feeble TV does its job
and passes the half-hour
A comfortable uneasy tiredness
being kept at bay.
An invite to a party loiters on the table
All those hapless, happy people
trapped on the dance floor
boogying away their problems
I sit at home repressed, depressed
feeling like lots of words with the
double S.
An anger about to implode.
Protect me from myself.
I look to the invite as my saviour
I go to the wardrobe
and put on my best clothes,
sit down on the couch
and vegetate.

A rant

There was always the other man. I knew that. I sometimes wonder what anyone sees in me and yet become disappointed if they're not committed to me fully. Is it just a game? She is so loving to me, she seems so loving towards everyone else too. I want full control. What is love? I don't know, I do the things I think loving people do, it's not natural. I feel my natural state is isolation, but only momentarily. I have to keep reminding myself I'm having fun. When she cries I comfort her but it's not from the heart or through compassion, it's just something I'm expected to do. I'm not a cold person but the warmth is concealed under layers and layers of bullshit. I'm not frightened to show my emotions and never lose my temper, I'm full of contradictions. I run the gauntlet from a safe distance, not really leading a life, more acting one. It's only when I'm alone that I enjoy the company of others. Not one person gives me all I need. Different people for different moods, not really leading a life, reading one. New people are exciting, the thing is not to overbear them with your friendship. Love flows more freely in a friendship and if you mess that up you can always become lovers. If you spend too much time with a woman eventually she won't give you the time of day, neither will your old friends, most of whom will settle down. This expression has always struck me as a bit of a giveaway that cohabiting is wrong. 'Settle down' implies the situation is not ideal, more it-will-have-to-do, yet it's the term we use when deciding to spend the rest of our lives with another. All negatives having pluses it's fortunate that by the time your mind has adjusted to such a lifestyle, these comments become redundant. Help! I'm running out of eligible bachelors, eventually I might find the right girl and I can get it all wrong with her as well. Maybe I should join a gym.

Shade

I feel tired and hungry
I eat some food, have a little nap
I feel tired and hungry
I continue to do all the things
I will always do
There's a nice pattern to my life
Out of the blue, I realize I've never had
a moment's happiness
Tears I didn't know I had, flood out
I want respite
A friend's kisses and concern have no effect
I don't know if it's her lips or my face
that is numb
I suppose it's a private moment
I cry harder, she starts to cry
And soon picturing this scene in our heads
we laugh hysterically,
and then cry some more
We go to bed together but alone
like a couple whose comfort
has displaced love
I dream of heavy people on my bed
and at any moment it's going to collapse
I feel awkward in every sense
I awake to find my t-shirt soaked through
More things inside me wanting to get out
In the morning I find I've lost interest
in many things
I've fallen down another rung
of the ladder
and I know I've got a fight
on my hands.

Dinner

VEG AND TWO VEG

A slight variation on the traditional family meal. It is a basic yet delicious, heavy meal to tide you over until the morning.

SERVES ONE
Ingredients

5 lb new potatoes (the small ones mind)
6 oz frozen peas
1 cheese and onion pie
salt
pepper
and that spicy stuff in your cupboard which is nearly out of date, so you'd better use it with everything from here on in

1 Wash spuds, put them in saucepan full of water, on full heat. Go in and catch the first half of *Happy Days*. When the ad break comes on, turn the potatoes down, say to them, 'No, I'm not going on a date with you,' (no, that's a little cookery joke). Really what you do is turn the heat down and fill new saucepan with water for peas.

2 On the packet of peas it states that you should wait until the water is boiling before you throw in the peas. I don't believe in this method, I think it's a Government ploy to pacify the voters. Their reasoning being if the people are busy they won't revolt. I say dunk the peas in straight away and don't worry about the simmering business. Go in and watch the rest of *Happy Days*.

3 Check the potatoes by sinking a fork in one, or if you have noticed there is no water left in the saucepan, they should be about ready. Drain if necessary.

4 At this stage, the peas should be flying all over the kitchen, turn off heat as they are just about ready.

5 Take pie out of fridge, undo the wrapper and eat cold.

6 Place pie in the middle of the plate, letting the potatoes circle it and pour peas over in a pot-luck kind of way. You can daub a bit of butter on plate for taste.

7 Treat yourself to a meal out some time.

SEX

*THE NEED
TO PUT PART
OF YOUR
BODY INTO
PART OF
SOMEONE
ELSE'S
BODY IN THE
NAME OF
LOVE*

Sweat

You get to know someone enough,
that you sleep together
Is it going to be that
'It's about time we had sex' time
Here goes, jump over the first hurdles of
touching, caressing, getting into the mood,
a man-made move
or to have spontaneous sex
where the sweat mingles and afterwards
you both look like you've just showered
It is so good you want to repeat it
it becomes a man-made move

After experiencing something so good
how come five minutes later you're the same
petty person
Have we lost the spirit, possibly to do
with too much religion
Out of man-made sex, what often results
is an embarrassed breakfast or an abortion
A hard penis will go anywhere
and this is how we men express our love
Yes the body rules the mind
and I don't think I can look a woman
straight in the crotch again.

Date with D

The tube journey was like any other tube journey I had experienced when high on a full stomach of Sunday anxiety. I had Flann O'Brien to keep me company. I knew he wouldn't throw another worry my way. When reading his book my mind wandered. So many people say his writings are hysterical, I seemed to be missing the joke. I read on regardless. I was surprised really that I kept so calm considering I was meeting the opposite sex. The battle was to ensue. We had talked twice before, once in the working place, that time I off-loaded my nerves with little witticisms, the other time behind the safety of a British Telecom line. I arrived in the rain at the bar. My date, I can't call her that, I think saying 'my night out with another mature adult' is more truthful to my mind, darted out of the blue looking very night-outish with another mature adult. So after a quick look at, in and around her face we walked into the bar. I bought the first drinks being brought up with that etiquette and started the conversation. Strangely she made me feel relaxed straight away. We broke common ground on lots of things and when I got around to my then obsessive subject of anxiety I knew she also suffered. Mind you, before I started getting attacks myself I was never aware of such things, now everybody I know seems to encounter them. It's a subject people don't like to bring up in polite conversation; our conversation was far from polite and as the night steamed ahead, I told little anecdotes of playing rock venues, slipping in jokes I wanted reactions to. Basically innocent stories from an innocent boy. She spoke of her two kids, fucking seventy-six-year-old men of the one leg variety, being spiked with heroin and general oddities. The tales became more interesting as time tightened up. I became looser with the drink, having a carefree attitude which I knew I didn't really have, but I was willing to deceive myself for the occasion. The pub was closing and this Australian-looking Australian came to clear our glasses. D suggested I might like some foreign-sounding food with my red wine, being easily led I was led away. Soon afterwards I find myself on a train sobering up, our chat had digressed to her telling me about the brutal slaying of her father, this was in between her asking every passenger on the train was it going our way. So now we're in the kitchen drinking. The only thing I was certain of was that she wasn't going to hand me a sleeping bag and point me to the couch. So why wasn't I petrified, the booze wasn't that strong. For some reason I still feel comfortable and I'm naked and I think I'm doing all the right things as I'm guided into that powerful experience called orgasm. And again I feel cheated. After our sexual explosion we have cigarettes and chat a bit more. She falls asleep and I'm left in this strange house with this strange woman thinking about nothing for hours. Then I decide it's time for another sexual explosion. I try to subtly wake her up and we go for it and afterwards I start to question whether or not she actually woke up for our second powerful experience. I lie awake for a while more, then sleep for two hours. In the morning I am told that it is quite unusual that her child didn't come in at the crack of dawn and lie beside her. 'She just feels her way around,' I'm told. I somehow don't think I would have been ready for that. Her other daughter comes in soon after to get a note for missing school. I feel like I'm in a TV movie and should be wearing a beard and a check shirt as I smoke endless cigarettes and stay upstairs like the dutiful husband when the man comes to fix the washing machine. I leave a few hours later when I feel an anxiety attack come on. After waiting a half-hour for the train on two hours' sleep, an empty stomach, ten cigarettes and a fair dose of self-hate, I figure maybe that's the reason for my anxiety attacks.

The smutty page

I think it's important that in every book there should be a bit of smut. A little section which turns the reader on. I remember as a teen thumbing through my mum's books, the ones hidden in the wardrobe, looking for the sexy bits. It was a real hindrance having to read the whole trashy novel just to find this piece. So, to save you the hassle, here is the smutty bit.

The scenario in these novels by the time they get to the sex scenes has usually gone something like this: the rugged good-looking type, Adam the gardener/errand boy, is having his fair share of problems. The old Duchess is trying to seduce him, she tries to blackmail him into having sex. The problem is, he is in love already. She goes out of her way to ruin this relationship. The Duke is sleeping with the maid just to keep things spicy. Adam has sworn to get his revenge. Out of the blue, the Duke and Duchess's daughter arrives for the weekend. They greet her as she gets off her pony. There's usually some spiel about how she has turned from being their little girl to full womanhood over the summer. Adam grabs her bags because that's his job. He is told to escort her to her room (this is another one of his menial tasks). The daughter, Prudence, wears her hair in a bun and has a near pretty face but her breasts defy gravity. On seeing her, Adam feels his loins tweak (this isn't one of his jobs). He sees revenge isn't far away. At this stage the book tends to give you an in-depth look inside our hero's head, but all you really need to know is that he is excited knowing that Prudence is still a virgin. He walks her to her room where she is to prepare before dinner. Adam notices her corset is fit to burst as her breasts push up for mankind. As they reach the room, Adam takes an instinctive gamble and kisses her full on the mouth. She resists faintly but he feels her heart flutter. Adam places her hand on the outline of his hard penis. She rummages around breathlessly. As Adam undoes her top he knows there is no stopping now. During these fumblings he realizes she is far from the inexperienced virgin she plays so well. She gently rubs the inside of his thigh, teasing his fast-filling balls, a rush of blood dizzies him as her breasts suffocate him whole. 'Suck hard,' she pleads. 'I don't want to ruin my appetite,' he says, toying with her. Without knowing how, she is completely naked, Adam fully clothed. He grasps at her boisterous bottom pretending they too are a pair of breasts. She is now gyrating on top of him. Adam feels like the Incredible Hulk as his trousers become two sizes too small around the crotch area. Her sex noises become more abrupt as he gloves her front, fingering delicately. He knows the second that she touches his throbbing member he will be able to put out all fires within a ten mile radius. She is screaming with excitement. 'How can one person make so much noise? Adam reasons. It is then he realizes they are not alone. 'How did the pony get in here?' Adam enquires. 'Go with the flow,' the Duke says. The Duchess is in a frenzy, multiple orgasms aplenty... I think you get the picture. I'm just going off for a quick shower. The novel finishes with Adam falling in love with Prudence, inheriting all the money. The pony sires a breed of top pedigree race horses and everyone lives happily ever after, except the Duchess who we find out was actually adopted. She becomes the maid but has quite a good sex life with the Duke from there on in. The reader goes to bed happy and horny.

REAL

LIFE

*THE THINGS
WE PUT UP
WITH IN
THE NAME
OF CIVILITY*

James

A child is born,
eyes open in disbelief
A child is dead,
eyes closed in disbelief
He cried when hungry
He cried when beaten to death
with an unknown weapon.
James was never to understand
the true horror of the world
He was spared this at least.
His parents must wonder why
the shops are still open,
why people are still having a good time,
why television still broadcasts,
so do I.
A twelve-year-old suspect must wonder why
his neighbours are baying for his blood,
when he did no wrong,
so do I.
We used to live in a civilized society
a society where now only the most
horrendous murders make the headlines
Think of the person somewhere in this country
being murdered as we speak
'That's terrible' we utter
And on we go with our business
Nobody's safe, nobody's blameless
                    Shame on us all.

England win the Grand Slam

I arrive in the pub
struggle to find a space
I notice a lot of rugby shirts
Lots of butch men kissing each other
After twenty minutes
I know there's going to be a fight.
People are trying to have a good time
Within the confines of our war-time licensing laws.
We push against each other
Soon the pub's atmosphere becomes background
As my company's conversation takes over
Suddenly the pushing
isn't in the name of England's victory.
it's a nuisance,
I look around and see
that dazed expression
The one that doesn't recollect anything but
can remember sitting innocently in the corner.
At this stage if there wasn't a fight
it would be a disappointment.
A butch man remembers kissing another butch man
and having no need for the rest of his pint
smashes it over him
One person's life ruined,
the rest of us having something to talk about.
Well done England.

Song lyrics for aspiring pop stars

This section is my way of helping any musically inclined person. Feel free to put any of these lines into your songs.

1 Hungry nights fulfil my days.

2 Will the real me please stand up yeah yeah yeah.

3 It's terrible being in love especially when you don't know with who.

4 I met two blokes and considered them friends, later I met some friends and considerated yeah yeah no.

5 I remember thinking that if she says no I will avoid the question and if she says yes I will avoid her.

6 So no more funny talks, twosome walks, held-out arm or misguided charm, she said you may not have the looks but you sure have character (you can end this with baby if it's a funky tune).

7 I write home saying I won't take handouts, just send some money.

8 In Dublin where they mass-produce saints and scholars, taking a sip of their cultured drink and lighting another taxed cigarette, not many people send postcards from Dublin.

9 With his elephant frame and mouse's heart and animal instinct, I'm all for cruelty to this creature.

10 It's about time he learnt to stand on his own four feet.

11 When you're away you get homesick, when you're there you get sick of home.

12 He was kicked from vanity's asshole with his last hitch to fashion as he turned twenty.

13 Not so much looking in awe, more awe, look at this.

14 I had one girl on my left and one on my right and another on my mind.

15 Yeah yeah yeah no baby yeah uh huh give it to me ooh yeah shooby doo bop a loola uh huh, don't vote Tory (repeat until bored).

The alcoholic

He sits with his pint
knowing he's going to hate himself
in an hour
We all like not to be ourselves at times
He is not stupid
He knows this is not the cure
But he can't see any other way out
He drinks more and more
He forgets he hates himself
He now hates the ones around him
Venom spews forth
Thoughtless, spur of the moment,
bubbles of slurred speech
hit out at the very core
of the minding-your-own-business type,
sitting within spitting distance of
the deranged drunk.
Now two people are hurt.
In the morning, what will later be termed
the all-is-forgotten-about conversation
is troubling the alcoholic
Yet it is wrong to feel sorry for him
This only digs a deeper hole.
Help him make the most
of what we've got
After all we're all going to end up
                        in that hole anyway.

The Continuation Of An Era

The country
slipped into
a tired apathy
on that Friday morning
Some people's life's work
put to bed,
others' just started.
The shocked,
how did it happen
expression
on broken people's faces
On Monday
the country
had returned
on to it's hunched back
teetering along
in a stop-starty way,
a few more cracks
showing through ...
The 'we'll deal with it later'
crowd
back in action.
And to think some people
didn't bother to vote.

Extremists

To understand loneliness, you have to spend time alone
To understand people, you have to back off
Moments or nights spent in isolation
Break the day-to-day conversation.
When given the chance
Different rules being no rules, means you rule
over the kingdom of nothingness
You find yourself caring
over careless creatures
giving a fuck for people
who don't give a fuck for themselves
My language can be excused and put to
the bottom of problems we concern ourselves with
It's frightening knowing nothing,
it's worse when you know a little

I feel like a stadium poet,
bombarding with bombastics
I want what you want
Something stops me,
just looking at things.
We all have our little concerns
which explode into
a way of life
and so you settle into an acceptance level
which you deem okay.
Extremists, I love you.

I want

'I think I'm suffering from exhaustion,'
said the girl thinking it was cancer
'I'll just do some blood tests,' said the doctor, exhausted
'Gulp,' said the girl, thinking this is serious
'You're a diabetic I'm afraid.'
'I'm afraid too,' said the girl
knowing now there was another trait to
her personality
She was a member of a new club
Certain things never again taken for granted
'You should know you can never drive
a bus or fly a plane,'
things she had never contemplated
'Would that worry you doc?' she asked
'I've never thought about it,' he answered straightly
'Never fly a plane, damn, I want to fly a plane.'
The girl was obsessed now.
'I need to fly a plane, I'm going to apply for
my licence tomorrow.'
'Calm down,' the doctor said.
'Is there anything you've ever wanted to do?'
cried the girl.
'Now that you mention it, I've always wanted
to swim with a dolphin.'
'What's stopping you?' she demanded
'I can't swim,' he said embarrassed

The girl came to terms with her illness.
The doctor took two weeks off,
came back with photos
to last a lifetime.

Swimming with dolphins

We all loaded off in our little pack
memories of normality fading
The thought of sharing the banter of
seventeen others, very frightening
I could just sit in my darkened room, again.
Surely the dolphins would bring us
together
The long drive to the seafront was accompanied
by some horrendous taped music
On first sight of the hairy sailor
their stringed dog and the deep sea
my room seemed comforting.
I fed the seagulls some chips,
made them dance for it mind.
The ocean was so clear
as everyone started to put on their
wet suits
I put mine on in the privacy of the
cabin's corner
Everyone buzzed with a half grin,
anticipating the excitement,
some brought cameras and videos
lessening the moment
for longevity
'The dolphins are coming,' said the captain
The eager ones jumped in
They came back like age-old hippies
certain phrases forever now part of their
vocabulary
Everyone got the chance to swim with
the dolphins
I, the non-swimmer, the frail old man
before his time,
got the chance to hang off a rope
breathing in salt
in panicked gulps.

It was enough for me to know the dolphins
were there,
I feel no need to touch
a metaphor for my life I thought
I noticed that every single person had
this fantastic grin on their face
looking so graceful in the water,
anything was forgivable!
This more so than seeing the dolphins
filled me with wonder
The story of the seal who thought
he was a dolphin,
refused to hang out with the other seals
filled me with wonder
I am the seal who likes to hang out
with the dolphins I thought
As I watched.
My watch was ruined from my little dip
Another metaphor for the timelessness of the day
Some felt sorry for me.
not being able to fully participate in the action
I went home, tired, damp, elated
The rest went off to chat about events
over fish and chips.

Nature

A bird's afterbirth lands on my balcony
A mother's utter despair ... perhaps
I look at it at regular intervals
over several hours
expecting somebody else to do something
about it
Maybe the mother is preparing some sort
of ceremony
or trying to get in touch with the father.
After a safe period of mourning
I grab a rubber glove
one with holes in it
I go downstairs and with my neighbour's
permission
bury it in his patch of dirt
I grab handfuls of this polluted soil
and making a small heap,
carefully place this little
ugly thing of beauty
into the ground
I wonder whether I should say a few words,
not being religious
I just rush back upstairs.
I feel pleased with myself
seeing all the cruelty heaped upon animals
at the hands of us so-called superior beings,
it was nice to show my respect
The next day I go about my normal
big-city life
Coming back from the shops I notice
the soil upheaved
and scattered on the concrete.
                    Nearby a cat is smirking at me.

Being Irish in London

'Oh, they're a chatty bunch'; 'the Irish are great talkers'; 'they're a very sociable breed of people.' These are things that Londoners say about the Irish. They may be right, but being Irish in London it is important to be sociable, to make your presence felt, to have an alibi when a bomb goes off. 'But your honour, I was watching the edited version of *The Late Late Show* on Channel 4.' Highly unlikely.

Being wrongly arrested is one of the drawbacks of having an Irish accent and a fancy shoulder bag. This is a little unfair to the police as it is not strictly the case. It is the poor working-class Irish who get accused; mind you, it is the poor working class, regardless of race, who get trodden on in caring London.

Class was never a big issue for me in Dublin, but if queried about it we were lower middle class/higher working class, depending on how much my father gambled over the weekend. John Major is always going on about wanting a classless society. I suspect he means he wants people to remain uneducated.

It is odd to see so many Irish living in London, considering that as children reading our history books we were taught to hate the British. In class the biggest insult you could throw at anyone was by calling them a Brit. Of course, absence makes the heart grow fonder so you can expect to hear bar-room republicanism in many an Irish ghetto over here. It is easy to understand nationalism, the geography of it makes sense, people want a united Ireland; for some the actual reasons are forgotten, just something to do with hatred. Being a Dub, we did not like people from Kerry; being a south Dub, I was supposed not to like people from north Dublin. This logic can go as far as hating your neighbours. At the end of the day, you can argue, is any piece of land worth a human life regardless of the reason?

It takes me back to a time when I was in Los Angeles in an Irish bar. A Dub living there for ten years chatted about his hatred for the British. When asked did he keep in touch with Ireland, he replied with no sense of irony, 'Yeah, I get the *News of the World* sent over every week.'

The British seem slightly more educated about Ireland now; years ago I was asked by a Londoner, 'What's it like when a bomb goes off?' All I could do was describe to the best of my knowledge scenes from *All Quiet on the Western Front.* Nowadays, as people living in London, regardless of origin, we are all under the threat of an IRA bomb; any one of us can become an 'unfortunate civilian casualty'.

Of course, there is a racism towards Irish people in general. Flying in from Dublin recently, I was stopped by a customs man who quite earnestly told me: 'Before I open the bag, you do know it is illegal to bring explosives into the country?' In this situation you want to say, 'Flip, I was never sure what your policy on explosives was, thanks for clearing that one up for me.' But, thinking of seven nights in a cell, I replied with a rather witty: 'Yes, I do.' It is odd. At the airport, people from Ireland and Jersey have to go through a security check first. They never seem to catch any members of the JRA in this way. The professional Irish, the 'we speak better English than the Queen herself' Irish, fit neatly in London. It is with thanks to the likes of Gabriel Byrne and Bob Geldof that a certain mystique has built up around the Irish – people love the Irish, people want to be Irish, they all have some connection with Ireland, anything from family to owning some Waterford glass and, boy, they can't wait to tell you about it.

Only yesterday, Steve Wright, the Radio 1 DJ, told me his grandfather was Irish. This to me is as interesting as telling me what he had for breakfast. Incidentally, it was bacon and eggs. I, like most people, feel you do not have to shout from the rooftops where you are from every five minutes, yet there is this oddly curious quest for Irishness in people. I would like to take the same people down the Holloway Road at two in the morning of a weekend and see how proud they are to be Irish then. This is where the people The Pogues used to glamorize, hang out. These are the people for whom their Irishness is the very core of their lives. Each culture has a horrible underbelly; this is Ireland's, a thuggery of lost souls, drinking themselves back to the homeland, releasing the frustrations of dead-end jobs, homesickness and a general apathy which they do not want to think about. As Pat Joyce says in the play *Patrick's Day*, they are the people 'who will do anything for Ireland except live there'.

Some might cry there are no jobs for them in Ireland; the fact is there are no jobs for anyone, anywhere, any more. They crave an Ireland that never existed. They have forgotten their reasons for leaving and now end up celebrating everything that is crap about our culture. The sad irony is they are not part of Irish culture any more, they are now part of British culture.

It frightens me when people come up to me and say, 'Those Saw Doctors are a great crack.' I start to panic that people are thinking this is what the Irish like, then the depression creeps up on you when you remember that they top the chart regularly in Ireland.

I do not want to be accused of snobbery. Some would argue the Saw Doctors say more to Irish people than Beckett ever did. Of course they do, but that is more an indication of the sadness of the times. When it comes to the arts I do not care how mindless it is as long as the makers put their heart and soul into it. I do not like the idea of ignorant people making money from masses of other ignorant people. It all amounts to taste at the end of the day, but I will not be happy until this is countered by the brilliant aspects of Irish culture seeping through. I would not mind getting up on the rooftops to shout out the names of the Fatima Mansions, A House, Emotional Fish, Paul Durcan, Dermot Bolger, Brendon Kennelly and Tom Murphy.

I feel it is of vital importance being Irish in London and more importantly as a human being, to help people think for themselves; people should not be frightened to go against the grain, they should not be frightened to say the Catholic Church is wrong, that governments are corrupt and that nationalism kills. I think it is the job of any person in the spotlight to try to give something back to society, not to cash in from it.

Seven jokes from my first set

Or how did I ever get this far

It should be pointed out at this point in my career, I used to wear a woolly hat on stage and speak in a deadpan sort of way.

1 It was always a bit sad going home to visit my parents, there was always tears at the doorstep but this time round they let me in.

2 I was down in Soho recently and this woman said 'If you give me £15 I'll show you a good time', (coy look from me) I gave her the money and she pointed to two people having an ice cream and said 'Look, they're having a good time.'

3 I was up in Camden market and I saw this guy and he wasn't wearing a leather jacket, I thought poser.

4 If you cast your mind back to the classroom, remember the little skinny fellow, sat up the front, absolutely everybody used to beat him up ... well he used to beat me up.

5 I think the most embarrassing thing that ever happened to me was I was having sex once, another embarrassing thing was ...

6 Those sex phone lines are a complete waste of time. Apparently.

7 I was at one of those student parties, you know the ones where you wake up still drunk with a strange pair of feet wrapped around your head. It wasn't until I got up to leave that I realized they were mine.

These all worked but the problem was they were all jokes, none of them true. After airing them about twenty times you just get bored, hence a lot of comics move on to the more self-discovery stuff, speaking the truth leaving the gags behind for the comics who see this as a job rather than a way of life.

The truth

We lie to each other on a daily basis
little white lies to stop embarrassment
big black ones to save face
Multi-coloured ones for the variety
We constantly can't face up to the
reality of ourselves
We escape through drugs, TV and religion
The truth seems shallow
we are shallow
we are empty
we are human
This is a foundation
knock it down
start again...
Then you can believe in you
and remember if you're looking for
something that big
it must be staring you in the face.

MOMENTS

*THAT'S ALL
LIFE CAN
EVER BE,
LET'S BE
GRATEFUL*

Happiness

Happiness is a faraway land
if you are far away it is home
it cannot be seen or heard
but has to be seen to be heard
be sure it has to be around the corner
hidden, obscured by fate

Happiness is good music sometimes
seeing someone smiling, nearly almost
when the bath water is just right,
a paragraph in a book
sleepy sensations on trains
an afternoon nap,
when beer goes down just right
a brilliant conversation, women,
mankind, a perfect cigarette,
the smell of petrol.
These all have their moments

Happiness is reflections
                    and looking forward to meeting you.

The clock goes back (Winter)

I feel very depressed, 'You feel depressed.'
Numb.
Not like from the dentist's injection.
You see people rushing home
in semi-darkness
I think everyone lives on their own
The bus driver is glad of our company
I read the Art page of the newspaper
The writer is passionate about stupid things
I watch television, it could be any night
Empty stomach pumped full of tea.
I have a cup of tea
I gaze over at the soaps, I go out
The pub is busy for a Monday night
I have a passionate conversation about stupid things
I wonder why. I drink.
Numb.
Not like from the freezing weather
Home.
Another day going through the motions
Numb.
I hope I awake tomorrow.

Mother

Mother you make me cry.
Always.
Because you've always been there for me
and yet we've never really spoken.
As if waiting for your death
to strike up a conversation
When we chat about your illness
you feel helpless
and I feel helpless
and I say the things you taught me
to say to ill people
and I cry and you cry
over your pain.
You're the only woman I never wanted
to sleep with.
And I constantly mourn your every
unhappy waking moment
What can I do?
When I come home,
I don't want to be there,
I block it out.
I escape you
only at a closer location
And every one of these lines makes me cry
I come home and try to explain myself
I get frustrated, which makes you frustrated.
Doesn't Dad come in handy then.

Shaking cream on Christmas Day while listening to Mary of the Fourth Form by the Boomtown Rats

Playing record
my Christmas present
shaking cream,
after turkey treat,
lid opens, cream spills,
Dad's jacket ruined
Dad's temper flares
record broken
Terrible Christmas.

Dad's version

Turn music down
Awful hangover
Sean shake cream
I'm starving
What happened?
You're sorry!
Jacket's ruined
My Christmas present
That'll teach you
Terrible Christmas.

One moment of silence please

'Will you marry me?' I asked. My eyes pleaded for some sort of reaction but all I got was a stunned silence followed by a hushed stillness which preceded a deafening quietness, until a socket of tranquility was ejected into the atmosphere. I tried to look at her. I knew it was not an easy decision. I myself had practised saying it into the mirror on several occasions and seeing what was in front of me I had my doubts. How could I ask someone to spend the rest of their life with me, when I wasn't sure what me entailed. But I'd thrown caution to the wind and now wanted it to blow away or hit me double force in the face. Thousands of thoughts became grains of sand in an outstretched hand, but the band played on, suddenly everything went quiet, where you could hear a pin drop, only one didn't. Momentarily a sense of déjà vu set in, but nobody could hear it. This moment was a result of my life in total. I was committed to this moment, little fears crept in, certain little niggling traits niggled away at my mind. Oh how could I spend my life with somebody who likes to wear brown corduroys and listens to Paul Simon and used to hang out with a TV personality. I had to stop myself before things got out of control, but then I remembered she looked a little like my mother.

What was keeping her? My destiny was being kept at bay and it didn't like this. My emotions were interacting with each other, regret became promise, promise became temperament, basically I didn't know what to think. I wouldn't be able to joke my way out of this one. I shouldn't have been so blunt and forthright, I could've said it differently. 'Do you fancy going off to the country for a dirty lifetime?' That would have made her laugh and weakened her power. I loved to see her laugh, in fact I loved nothing better, but I was only twenty-three and had never even been skiing and there are certain wines I still haven't tasted. Maybe there is a woman out there, bring her in, let us mingle, then I will decide, but it's not my decision, it's hers. I wish I could take it all back now. I don't want to marry her, it would never work, we would take each other for granted, love would last two or three years maximum, another year of contentment, but that's four years shared, away from the pitifulness of my own existence. Away from all the what-could-have-beens, the responsibilities towards my own sanity. Then waking up each morning with somebody beside you until that fateful day when you realize you had mistaken hate for love. She wants to kiss and cuddle, you want to kick and struggle, you feel soft and sloppy, she feels like another cup of coffee. I was here waiting for a reply to my indecent proposal. At that moment a vacuum seemed to suck away at every noise until the whole room felt like the inside of a jam jar, empty, still, silent . . . but with no jam. At this stage the calmness of the moment had built up to the point of no return and I expected the feedback of it all to set in but instead it expanded until the serenity of it all was fit to burst. It was as if this peacefulness had amassed over a period of time. She remained tight-lipped as if mute. There was a lull. I was speechless. Mum wasn't the word. 'No,' she said.

Outburst

Men continually flexing their muscles
Women who want to sleep with Arnold Schwarzenegger
People who talk with cocaine
People waiting by the phone
Ones who watch *Blind Date*
A moralistic American sit-com
Poets who tell the truth... momentarily
These are all modern day illnesses

Madness calls on me,
it doesn't want me to play with it
it wants me to hide under my bed
frightened of my own mind

Why do we pretend otherwise
We're capable of good and bad
Does the Pope imagine the nakedness of a pretty girl
or am I truly sick

We build a close circle of friends
to trap ourselves with
Security can be so scary

Should we walk around with labels
to categorize ourselves
Warnings to strangers on how we should be
handled
like we were all over-sized cardigans

Apologies to all and sundry.

The beautiful girl dancing

Again I find myself in a late-night bar
Losing it big time
I see the beautiful girl dancing
Others are gyrating to songs
they're not really listening to.
Animals
I see others habitually drinking
their next beer
The barman cynical to their rudeness
I see me standing there,
being counted as one of them.
Earlier in the natural sunlight
I fed parrots with bird seed
from my hand,
tame, beautiful, well-fed
lazy birds
but yes i bought it
Just as they did.
And again I find myself surrounded
by morons
I want to kiss the world goodbye
What keeps me alive . . . hope.
And to watch the beautiful girl dancing.

The beautiful girl stops dancing

The beautiful girl stops dancing
and we are within coy looks
distance of each other.
I embrace the excitement of the
moment
I fall in love with that moment
It's like a flash
I've realized I will forever fall
in love with those moments
Others will dismiss me
as I dismiss them
I will not defend myself
I will continue to make the same
mistakes
Only now with this new
knowledge
I'll keep enjoying those moments
You'll enjoy your relationships
I bid you good luck
Love is so complicated
Especially when there are two people
involved.

The gift

A man in his early thirties collects the post from his hallway, the rain is pelting at the door, it seems to be coming in at every direction. When he opens his letter, it is revealed to be a birthday card – a beautiful card with an array of multi-coloured kites on it.

CUT TO

Late at night, and a slow-moving camera tracks across an urban landscape to reveal a high-rise block: there are a few odd lights on in some of the flats and the camera tracks into the young boy's bedroom. He is wide awake, excited about his birthday. In his hand he has a tatty old kite, held together with bits of string and Sellotape. The light goes out and the rain starts.

CUT TO

Early the next morning the rain relentlessly pours down. The boy is determined to fly his kite with his father. The father is slumped on a chair in the tiny lounge watching the horse-racing on the television, he is engrossed. The boy's mother is getting on with her Saturday chores, she is fuming as the rain is keeping her from putting out the washing.

The flat is very cramped and the three characters are constantly getting in each other's way.

They appear to the viewer to be on display, as if they are in a zoo. It is the boy's story so the focus will always be on him and how he relates to what is happening around him. Most of the information will be got across through the boy's mumblings (and the older man's memories in voice-over).

The three characters are studied individually as the tension rises due to the relentless rain. In the background there will be the constant, driving rain beating harder and harder.

The young boy becomes more and more frustrated stuck indoors, he continually pesters his dad to take him out. His dad at this stage has three horses up on his accumulator, the mother pounds away with the hoover, she keeps asking them to put their feet up, the hoover is affecting the TV reception, the dad is trying to underplay his winning ways in front of his wife, the young boy is starting to throw his kite up in the air in the flat.

The humidity is rising, the pace is quickening and the three characters are becoming more and more agitated with each other. Tension mounts as the last race starts: the father is on the edge of his seat, the mother hoovers and the boy is tearful by now. The rain is attacking the block and damp starts to appear inside.

As the race finishes, the hoover, by now stuffed full, bursts, and dust erupts all over the floor. The mother is beside herself. The father wins his race and in his excitement tramples on the boy's kite, but he says with his winnings they'll go out now and get the best kite ever. The mother hassles her husband about his winnings, the boy hassles his father about how big his new kite will be and then from the TV screen we suddenly hear of a steward's enquiry.

The father loses. The boy, knowing the implications of what has happened, quietly shuts himself in his room. He can hear his parents shouting next door. Nobody notices that the rain has suddenly stopped. The boy patiently begins to piece together his kite as the camera tracks towards his window. Suddenly, against the grey, wet urban horizon, a rainbow appears and lands in the boy's bedroom filling it with multi-coloured light. The boy runs to his window and much to his delight, he sees that the sky is full of assorted multi-coloured kites flying.

THE END

The clock goes forward (Summer)

Bright evenings, dust down the sunglasses
change the mood on the Walkman
listen to an uplifting tune
and the world's a great fucking video
Even the omnibus version of *Brookside*
makes me happy,
well not happy,
well all right It's as depressing as ever.
As ever I dream of living in a big house
in the country,
kids holding on to my thighs,
a faithful dog eager for its walk,
by my side
and six cans of Coke in the fridge
which I can open at my own discretion
My wife is pondering around, day-dreaming
her own day-dream
somewhere else in the house
I feel healthy,
my work builds up an appetite,
I look out yonder at the green fields,
alone now,
all attachments having their little
private moments elsewhere
I see a just world beyond those fields,
I reflect on sadder times

and I don't recoil
I grow steadier, my back becomes upright
not through a well-disciplined schooling
but with ascension into relaxation
A new sensation starts engulfing my body,
I become frightened,
this is always the way,
when we encounter something new.
I go with it
I now know freedom.
The old me would have thought this high
would be countered with a crushing, breathtaking down.
Those spoiling tactics.
But this is too good
to be false, this is true.
This is a perfect moment.

The object of your affection becomes distorted after use?

So why trust impulse, when one impulse soon takes over from the last. Yet you can't weigh every situation otherwise different impulses would out balance each other and you will end up doing nothing eternally. Therefore reflecting on the past you pick and choose your impulses, keeping a check on them at regular intervals, but never enough to make you constantly aware of each one. And, so when you come to the point of deciding on a way of life, on picking out a philosophy, you never make this decision in the mood of the moment, that impulse. Having said that, your state of mind will affect the way you reflect. Leaving you never fully aware of anything.

People busy themselves looking for happiness, this is an impossibility, happiness is a state of mind not a way of life. It can only ever last for a moment and you can never be aware of it at the time. Relaxation is often seen as a sleeping partner to happiness. You can attain and throw aside happiness by the use of discipline. You can discipline yourself to what you will or won't do. You can assess your situation, ask yourself questions. Do I do all I can as a socialist, do I never compromise? This seems too regimented. You could take on board your ideals against the situation and you can conclude that there will be certain compromises within your principles. But you never have to compromise on that.

Why are there so many public philosophies? You air a view in the hope that somebody will agree with it, when really philosophy concerns how you feel as an individual. I would say find your own philosophy and then keep it to yourself. But remember to try to live by it as well or the whole exercise becomes pointless.

The individual has no place in modern society, we're expected to cohabit, interrelate as a race. Sex is our form of communication. Sex ends in climax. The climax is reached with the satisfaction of that moment coupled with the relief that it's over. A rush of adrenaline is often mistaken for pleasure. If you realize what's coming and you're basically going for that goal, the only pleasure can be that it will somehow be better. If we put this in perspective, realize what's in store, can we then not relish all of the sensations including the down side and appreciate that as part of the experience? You can take relief that you know what the pleasure is without ever having to succumb to it. Within this process there will always be pain and pleasure. Pain is always compensated for by the knowledge that soon there will be less pain. A deep wound heals itself, that's pleasure, that's happiness. Pleasure is impossible if pain doesn't exist. In conclusion, climax is almost always followed by anti-climax, we know this so can never fully enjoy anything in that respect. The only consolation being pain is also impossible if pleasure doesn't exist so we can never be fully immersed in pain either. I must definitely join a gym.

Wrecking the wreck

Breathing heavy
not being able to lift anything heavy
putting shit up my nose
soaking my liver
aches and pains
not eating properly
vegetating
staying indoors
smoking beyond the enjoyment threshold
hardly any sleep
weak-kneed, weak-willed
constantly.
These are a few of my favourite things.